T0114304

Praise for *The Intelligent Negotiator*

"Charles Craver is that welcome rarity—a leading academic who possesses a sure grasp of the practicalities of everyday negotiating. And unlike many of his peers, Craver is not embarrassed about making a good deal for his side of the table."

—James C. Freund, author of *Smart Negotiating*

"An excellent guide to obtaining your negotiating goals. For those wanting to achieve better results at the bargaining table, this is an invaluable resource."

—Andrew M. Kramer, partner,
Jones Day Reavis & Pogue

"I rely often on the powerful insights of Professor Craver. He fully appreciates the subtleties of the process of negotiation. I hope my adversaries don't read this book."

—Lon Babby, attorney for professional athletes

"Charles Craver goes beyond the traditional approaches to bargaining. Read this book and you will dramatically enhance your negotiating skills."

—Ambassador John W. McDonald, chairman,
Institute for Multi-Track Diplomacy

"Charles Craver imparted invaluable lessons in the art of negotiation in the course I took from him thirty years ago. *The Intelligent Negotiator* is a must-read for anyone looking to maximize his success in competitive business. It brims with compelling strategies for achieving superior results."

—Leigh Steinberg, sports attorney and CEO,
Assante Sports Management

THE INTELLIGENT
NEGOTIATOR

*What to Say, What to Do,
and How to Get What You Want—
Every Time*

CHARLES CRAVER

 THREE RIVERS PRESS · NEW YORK

Published by Three Rivers Press, New York, New York.
Member of the Crown Publishing Group, a division of Random House, Inc.
www.crownpublishing.com

Originally published in hardcover by Prima Publishing, Roseville, California, in 2003.

This book is not intended as a substitute for professional, legal, or financial advice. As laws may vary from state to state, readers should consult a competent legal or financial professional for more detailed advice. In addition, readers should understand that the business world is highly dynamic and contains certain risks. Therefore, the author and publisher cannot warrant or guarantee that the use of any information contained in this book will work in any given situation.

Library of Congress Cataloging-in-Publication Data
Craver, Charles B.
    The intelligent negotiator : what to say, what to do, and how to get what you want—every time / Charles Craver.
        p.   cm.
    Includes bibliographical references and index.
    1. Negotiation. I. Title.
BF637.N4.C74   2002
302.3—dc21   2002066304

ISBN 978-1-4000-8149-3

145052501

CONTENTS

ACKNOWLEDGMENTS

I t is impossible to prepare a book on negotiating without relying upon the theories and concepts articulated by experts from diverse fields of study, including communication, psychology, sociology, law, and business. Those scholars have enhanced my understanding of the negotiation process. I also thank the hundreds of students who have taken my Legal Negotiating course and the thousands of lawyers and businesspeople who have participated in my Effective Legal Negotiation and Settlement programs, providing me with new insights and interesting bargaining stories.

I am especially indebted to Beth Lieberman, who took my original manuscript and patiently and professionally turned it into a finished work. Her extraordinary editorial assistance significantly enhanced the final product. Thanks to Ruth Younger for her extraordinary copyediting talents. My project editor, Michelle McCormack, further enhanced the final work. I must also thank David Richardson of Prima Publishing for giving me the opportunity to bring my ideas and teachings to a broader readership, and for his deft guidance throughout the publishing process.

My sincere gratitude goes to my agents, Janet Rosen and Sheree Bykofsky, who had confidence in the book I sought to produce.

I must finally thank Katey, my loving spouse and negotiating partner for the past thirty-five years. She, more than anyone, has taught me more about the mutual benefits to be achieved through effective negotiating.

INTRODUCTION

I ntelligent Negotiators are prepared, confident, and supremely effective. They know what to expect of each unfolding stage of a bargaining encounter. They have defined their own goals and determined how they can best attain them; they have also discerned the goals of their counterparts. Intelligent Negotiators' vast knowledge of bargaining techniques allows them to create powerful negotiating strategies that advance their side's interests and at the same time enhance the final outcome for everyone involved.

The goals of the Intelligent Negotiator are often work-related. Who's going to cover the client meeting in Omaha? Should we charge our usual 10 percent commission on the contract for a particular client, or reduce it to 7 or 8 percent to ensure future client loyalty? What quality guarantees should we get from the raw material supplier we're thinking of using? Should I insist on being given the executive title of the person I'm replacing, or wait until I've demonstrated my capabilities in the new position?

At other times, the subject of negotiation is personal or professional. How can I land the perfect job that just became available? How can I get the starting salary I feel I deserve? How can I get the salary increase I think is appropriate? Can I get my superior to change negative comments in my last performance evaluation? How can I interact more effectively with my coworkers and subordinates?

Still other issues relate to family and quality of life. Where will our family go for summer vacation? Can we get better terms on the second mortgage we are taking out to pay for our child's college education? How can we minimize the cost of car or appliance repairs? Negotiating is the key to finding the best solution in each of the above situations.

NEGOTIATING OUR WAY THROUGH LIFE

Although most of us rarely stop to think about it, we negotiate our way through life. Every day we negotiate with family, friends, members of our communities, business associates, salespeople, and complete strangers. Still, many of us are uncomfortable with the idea of bargaining. We dread the psychological battle of wills, the exploitive rituals, and the deception it normally entails. We tell ourselves that bargaining is not a normal part of life, even believing that most things in life are not negotiable. We go to stores, examine the price tags on desired commodities, and decide whether to purchase those items at the stated prices. We rarely seek more beneficial terms, fearing we will embarrass ourselves by even asking. If we only realized how many salespeople in even staid retail establishments are willing to negotiate lower prices or other customer-beneficial terms when asked, we could benefit dramatically.

Businesspeople often fail to appreciate the degree to which they must negotiate with superiors, subordinates, and others in the employment setting. They cavalierly arrange employment relationships, supplier contracts, and customer deals without recognizing the bargaining aspects—and potential enhanced rewards—of these critical encounters.

Some less-proficient negotiators excuse their lack of interest in the bargaining process by maintaining that objective market-driven forces determine the price or value of most commercial—and many non-commercial—items. They think they have no control over "externally regulated" factors. This assumption completely ignores the personal—and necessarily subjective—factors that affect bargaining encounters. A prospective car or home buyer who wants a particular car model or a specific house that is in demand is likely to pay a premium. On the other hand, someone who is willing to purchase a different car or house can offer a lower bid that may result in saving literally thousands of dollars. People with new job offers who ask for higher starting salaries get paid substantially more than those who merely accept the initial offers. Even department store shoppers who negotiate prices may save 10 to 20 percent over shoppers who pay the stated prices for the items they purchase. Buyers who politely ask sales clerks "Is this the best price you can give me?" may receive last week's sales price or be offered a discount if they purchase two of the items they are considering.

Skilled negotiators realize that various factors—beyond basic seller cost—play a significant role in bargaining encounters. These diverse factors determine the *settlement range* (see figure 1). As each side prepares for a negotiation, its participants consider the relevant objective considerations: the monetary cost of specific items, the opportunity costs associated with the trading of one

employment situation for another, or the value of anything else we may be thinking of exchanging for other
benefits. The other side makes similar calculations with
respect to the relevant items from its perspective. Each
party determines the most it will pay or the least it will
accept to enter into the exchange being contemplated.
The overlap between the parties' respective bottom lines
(represented by the shaded area in figure 1) defines the
settlement range. Every point within that range is acceptable to both of the negotiating parties.

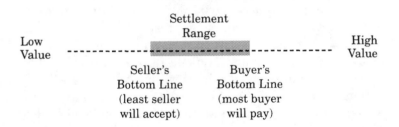

Figure 1. Settlement Range.

Once the participants begin their bargaining interaction and move toward the settlement range, the objective
considerations become less significant, and subjective factors begin to influence party behavior. How much does
each side want the deal? How risk-averse or risk-taking
is each participant? What occurs *within the settlement
range* is a psychological battle of wills. If one side can convince the other that the other must move in its direction,
the other party will do so. Different individuals agree to
very different terms with respect to seemingly identical
transactions because of the various subjective factors influencing the interactions.

Several years ago in my work as a negotiations consultant, I became involved in a personal-injury negotiation. The plaintiff had been injured, and his attorney wrote a letter to the insurance company demanding $100,000. After that figure was rejected, the plaintiff decided to retain the attorney with whom I work. We developed a strong negotiating position and settled the $100,000 case for *more than $500,000!* Our efforts greatly benefited the plaintiff, and was costly to an insurance firm that should have recognized the reasonableness of the original $100,000 demand and settled the case quickly.

Individuals who appreciate the basic factors that influence all interpersonal transactions obtain more satisfactory results than those who do not. They know how to prepare for these exchanges, they understand the crucial verbal and nonverbal communication skills involved, and they appreciate the different negotiating games being played. They know when to take a hard position and when to adopt a more conciliatory approach.

Becoming an Intelligent Negotiator allows you to create situations of opportunity for yourself and your negotiating counterparts. The people across the table possess the capacity to improve our situation, which is why we are talking with them. Both parties believe that a successful transaction will enhance their present circumstances. If superiors and subordinates can agree on work assignments and performance expectations, their relationships will flourish. If buyers and sellers of goods and services can establish trusting relationships, both sides will benefit. If these people are unable to agree upon their many interdependent issues, their relationships will suffer.

One of my recent bargaining encounters demonstrates the benefits to be derived from negotiating opportunities. I arrived at a hotel in Atlanta at which I had a guaranteed reservation. The clerk indicated that he had no room because of an unusual number of holdovers who had not departed as scheduled. He offered to relocate me to another hotel, but I asked if he had anything available. He said he had half a suite containing a single bed. I said this would be acceptable, but suggested that the $175 price for the room I had reserved would be excessive for the accommodations he was providing. I was then silent and awaited a response from him. I expected a reasonable price reduction and was surprised when he offered me the smaller room on a complimentary basis. I was glad I had not made the first offer, because I would have suggested something in the $100 to $120 range!

THE RITUALISTIC NATURE OF NEGOTIATING

Most people detest the ritualistic nature of bargaining encounters. Why don't negotiators say what they really think? Why must they employ disingenuous games that seem designed to exploit others? Why do we spend substantial amounts of time discussing seemingly irrelevant considerations such as traffic, weather, sports, politics, and mutual acquaintances before we begin to focus on the fundamental issues involved? Why can't we simply state at the outset what items we want and what we are willing to give up to obtain those items?

Ritualistic aspects are inherent to most bargaining interactions for several reasons. When people begin a negotiating encounter, they are anxious—even when they interact with friends or acquaintances. They don't know whether amicable agreements can be achieved, nor do they know the actual terms to be agreed upon. If both parties begin in a stressful state, they will encounter difficulties that may preclude mutual agreement. By taking the time to establish some rapport and create a more positive negotiating environment, they greatly enhance the probability of a pleasant and productive interaction.

Gerry Williams, a negotiation scholar and teacher at Brigham Young University Law School, spent several years in Afghanistan, where all consumer goods are negotiable. He had to barter for fruits, vegetables, meat, poultry, breads, and so on. He regularly went through the same ritual with the potato merchant, asking, "How much are the potatoes?" He was told they were 12 afs per kilo. He replied that they didn't look too good, and offered 2 afs. The merchant countered with 10, Gerry with 4, the merchant with 8, and Gerry with 6, which was accepted.

One day, Gerry decided to avoid this ritual and directly offer 6 afs for his potatoes. He went down early and watched a woman go through the usual 12, 2, 10, 4, 8, and 6 afs exchange. He then placed 6 afs on the counter and asked for a kilo of potatoes. The merchant said they were 12 afs. When Gerry said he had been paying 6 afs for weeks, the merchant replied that there had been a drought in the North causing the price of potatoes to rise. Gerry then reminded the merchant of the sale to the woman ahead of him for 6 afs, but was told that deal was a "mission of mercy." That woman had recently lost her husband and had to feed a number of small children. He thus took a loss on that sale.

Gerry spent more time on that day with the merchant than on any other occasion, and he left with no potatoes. The merchant was not willing to sell for Gerry's opening offer of 6 afs because that would be an insult, and Gerry was not willing to pay more than the 6 afs he had become accustomed to paying. Gerry returned the following morning and asked: "How much are the potatoes?" Gerry finally appreciated how crucial ritualistic behavior is to negotiating interactions.

During the preliminary portion of a bargaining encounter, the participants are sizing one another up. Each side wants to ascertain information regarding the other side's personal and professional background, its negotiating experience, the external options that may be available to the other side, and the degree to which it needs the items being exchanged. Individuals who ignore the importance of these preliminary discussions are likely to provide their opponents with beneficial information that they may subsequently use against them.

When you engage in the bargaining process, let it develop deliberately. Realize that it takes time for nervous participants to begin to feel comfortable with these encounters. Impatient negotiators are doubly cursed. Ironically, the more they rush a negotiation, the longer it takes. The stages break down and have to be repeated. In addition, the more impatient negotiators hurry a bargaining encounter, the less efficient the distribution will be of the items being exchanged due to the lack of cooperative bargaining. Patient negotiators who permit the process to develop slowly achieve both faster and better overall results.

The second bothersome factor in negotiating situations is the frequent deception involved. Someone willing to pay $21,000 for a particular car does not begin an encounter with the salesperson by disclosing this figure, nor does the salesperson, who is perfectly willing to sell the vehicle for $19,800, initially disclose that price. The buyer and seller engage in an awkward dance during which each tries to get the other to state a specific monetary figure. The salesperson emphasizes the $22,500 sticker price, while the potential buyer mentions the $19,000 dealer cost. After a seemingly interminable exchange of incremental concessions, the parties agree on a price in the $20,000 to $20,500 range—satisfying the underlying interests of both sides. Although the exchange might have been more pleasant and less stressful had the parties agreed upon this price at the beginning, participants usually can't do so. They must understand that, without the ritualistic testing of each side's resolve and the preliminary disclosure of disingenuous positions, the buyer cannot determine how low the dealer may be willing to go, and the salesperson can't tell how much the buyer may be willing to pay. Those who ignore the bargaining aspects of such an interaction are likely to pay their $21,000 limit— and some may even be induced to go $500 to $1,000 above that benchmark.

When the car dealer begins the initial discussions by saying "I cannot go below the $22,500 sticker price," and the prospective purchaser begins by saying "I will not go above the $19,000 dealer cost," have they engaged in reprehensible dishonesty? Most people who consider this issue carefully are likely to answer "no." A truthful individual is not a person who always tells the truth, but a person who tells the truth when the truth is expected. Most of us would not consider it dishonest to compliment a colleague's new outfit or hairstyle though we do not find it attractive, or to falsely tell an acquaintance we have another engagement when asked to attend a dinner we would prefer to avoid. We recognize that a truthful response would be considered needlessly cruel.

When we negotiate, some deception is expected— especially when we engage in commercial discussions or business dealings. Each side wants to induce the other to believe it must provide more generous terms than are required to consummate the deal. As a result, we don't anticipate entirely candid responses to questions about price or value. We expect some "puffing" and "embellishment," so long as these statements don't go completely beyond the bounds of reality. We expect car dealers to emphasize sticker prices, and car salespeople assume that experienced buyers will focus on dealer costs. Both will indicate an unwillingness to go much above or below these benchmarks. The salesperson will stress the $1,000 retail price of the advanced sound system in the vehicle being discussed (which actually cost the dealer $600), while the prospective buyer will disingenuously suggest no interest in such an expensive item. So long as these misstatements pertain to such things as our true settlement intentions and the value we place on the different items being exchanged, the dissembling will be tolerated. Only when the misrepresentations concern issues we have the right to know do claims of dishonesty arise. For example, if a car dealer claimed that a vehicle had side air bags when it only had front air bags, or stated that a six-cylinder engine had eight cylinders, such misstatements would be considered unethical and even fraudulent.

Intelligent Negotiators know the difference between expected puffing and embellishment—and improper deceit. They realize the critical degree to which personal integrity affects their ability to negotiate effectively. Most bargaining exchanges are made orally, in person or on the telephone, with the participants relying on the factual information being exchanged. If people lost their reputation for honesty when truth-telling was expected, they would greatly undermine their ability to negotiate. Everything they said would have to be verified, and all agreements would have to be reduced to writing and signed. The bargaining process would become cumbersome and inefficient. If you ever contemplate the overt misrepresentation of pertinent information, remember the degree to which such dishonesty will affect your future interactions if discovered.

By reading this book, you will learn the definitive stages and techniques of the negotiating process. The first section details the necessary preparation before you even get to the table: Be familiar with common negotiating styles and understand which one you should use, define your bottom line, determine what your counterpart's bargaining power is, establish firm aspiration levels for yourself, prepare your opening offer, and choreograph the sequence of events.

The second section shows how to build rapport, create value, and claim value during the stages in which participants size one another up, exchange basic information, then determine who gets what. You will learn how to ascertain information regarding the other side's personal and professional background, their negotiating experience, the external options that may be available to them, and the degree to which they need the items being exchanged. You will also learn how to shape the pie, support your positions in the strongest possible way, plan your concession strategy, and deal with various bargaining ploys you encounter.

The third section provides dozens of negotiating techniques, methods to firmly close the deal, and ways to expand the pie with cooperative bargaining to maximize the results achieved by the bargaining participants.

The final section contains practical applications of techniques to negotiating employment situations, buying cars and houses, and dealing with repair shops.

You may believe you are already an effective negotiator because of your advanced educational training, or you may fear that you are an ineffective bargainer because you lack formal education. In more than thirty years of teaching negotiation courses, practicing law, and mediating disputes, I have found no correlation between negotiating proficiency and educational attainment. Good students and good negotiators possess different mental skills. Successful students possess high abstract-reasoning skills represented by elevated IQ scores, while adept negotiators possess advanced interpersonal skills—what brain-researcher and consultant Daniel Goleman calls *emotional intelligence*.[1] Intelligent Negotiators know how to prepare for the negotiating exchanges, they understand the crucial verbal and nonverbal communication skills involved, and they appreciate the different games being played.

My goal is to help you develop the skills to become a more proficient negotiator. When you learn the definitive stages and practice the techniques, you will find that every negotiation—whether personal, professional, or organizational—looks different to you than it once did. Your bargaining encounters will be more manageable, and you will appreciate the fact that they represent opportunities for you and your counterparts.

FELICIA BROWN'S EMPLOYMENT QUEST

The story of job-seeker Felicia Brown will appear throughout this book. Her hypothetical situation illustrates the techniques in each chapter.

Felicia and Bill Brown are in their early thirties. Married for ten years, they have a seven-year-old son and a five-year-old daughter. When they first met eleven years ago, both Bill and Felicia were teaching high school science in Smallville. Four years ago, Bill left teaching for a scientific position with the State Environmental Protection Agency office in Smallville, for which he is currently earning $52,000 per year. Three years ago, Felicia earned her Master's Degree in computer science and network management and has since been teaching computer science courses to eleventh and twelfth grade students. She has also helped manage her school district's computer network. She is presently earning $42,000 per year.

Bill has been offered a supervisory position with the State EPA in Metropolis, the State capital. His salary would increase to $57,000, and he and Felicia would be able to relocate near both sets of parents who live in Metropolis suburbs. Felicia has been thinking of leaving teaching for a network manager position with a small retail firm located in the Metropolis area. If Bill and Felicia are to relocate, Felicia must obtain a job offer from one of the several retail companies that have current network manager openings, and she must negotiate her new employment terms.

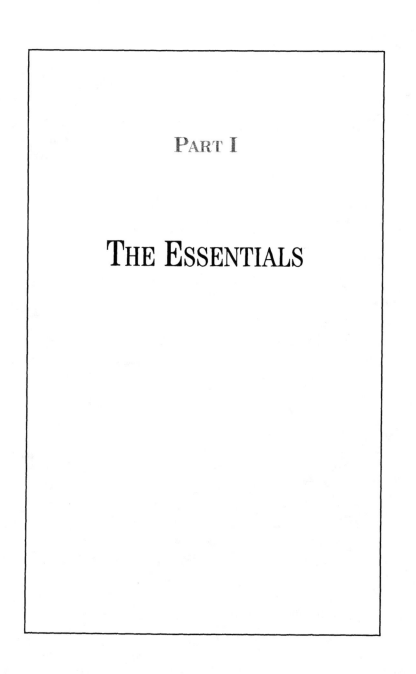

PART I

THE ESSENTIALS

CHAPTER 1

NEGOTIATING STYLES

D on't even try to adopt just one negotiating style or philosophy, for there is *no single* approach that can effectively govern *all* bargaining transactions. Whether negotiating with family, friends, business and professional associates, service providers, or community bodies, people conduct themselves differently in each and every negotiation, depending on their relationship to the other party involved.

The more distant the relationship between the parties, the "harder" the bargaining will be. Consumer purchases are excellent examples of this because they are among the most impersonal of our negotiations—typically one-time encounters with people who are, more often than not, strangers. Purchasing big-ticket items such as cars or houses beautifully illustrates transactions in which we not only lack ongoing personal relationships with our bargaining counterparts, but are also dealing with sophisticated sellers—or their proficient dealers and agents. Here most of us believe that *caveat emptor* (buyer beware) rules should apply.

When we negotiate with business and professional associates or community bodies, we are acting within already existing relationships that we plan to continue, or may hope to develop a relationship with a regular contact. In such situations, it is best to seek mutually beneficial results that satisfy the basic needs of *both sides*. For example: One of your employees has procured a job offer from another company and tells you that, if you match the salary the other firm offered her, she will reject that offer and stay with you. You very much want to keep this employee, so you give her the salary increase plus additional job responsibilities. This solution satisfies your budget constraints, maintains equilibrium in the department, and allows your employee to advance her career and remain at her preferred firm.

Negotiations with family and friends are our most intimate negotiations. They usually require cooperative behavior to achieve mutually beneficial goals and maintain harmony. For example, a married couple might relocate to Chicago because the husband will attend graduate school there. They decide, however, to rent an apartment in a neighboring suburb because the wife prefers to live close to her place of work rather than right in the university community.

Negotiators, whether bargaining with friends or strangers, are apt to use a particular style during their encounters. The following sections define and describe the relative merits of three negotiating styles.

COMPETITIVE-ADVERSARIAL STYLE

As a participant in dozens of labor negotiations, I have seen company agents open the bargaining with their employees' representatives with something like this:

MANAGEMENT: We've reviewed the situation and conclude that $X is a fair price for your services.

LABOR: That does not come close to the value our people add to your operation.

MANAGEMENT: This is what the services themselves are worth to us, and that is all we intend to pay for them. Take it or leave it.

The management negotiator above is a Competitive-Adversarial negotiator. Competitive-Adversarial negotiators (or "Adversaries") are win-lose participants who see a fixed pie: the more of the pie that I get, the less you get (and vice versa). Because Adversaries always want to leave the table with the biggest bag of marbles, they are fierce in their bargaining. An Adversary views your gain as his or her loss. This is why Adversaries are so often untrusting and manipulative. For instance, at some point in the negotiation, an adversarial management representative will step forward and raise the employees' compensation, without giving a clue that he or she plans to do this. The adversary's strategy is to put the counterpart on the defensive by being hostile, aggressive, and inflexible, and to move toward the other side only when forced to do so. This style of negotiating is also known as power bargaining or hard bargaining.

If you are negotiating with an Adversary, you can expect your counterpart to do the following:

- Begin with low offers and/or high-level demands.
- Minimize the disclosure of relevant information.
- Focus principally on his or her stated positions rather than reason out solutions with you.
- Make minimal concessions.
- Employ threats to intimidate you.
- Seek to maximize his or her own return at all costs.

Adversaries behave competitively with all opponents, seeking optimal results for themselves. With this zero-sum mentality, they miss benefits and opportunities that can be achieved through jointly expanding the pie.

COOPERATIVE–PROBLEM-SOLVING STYLE

Other company agents use an approach similar to the following:

SUPPLIER: I've got a problem. I cannot guarantee delivery of your computer chips on March 15th.

ACCOUNT: Why is that?

SUPPLIER: My production supervisor went into the hospital and won't be back until next month. I have an interim supervisor and three additional crews to work on this around the clock, but we still might not make the date.

ACCOUNT: You let me know well ahead of time, which is somewhat of a help, John. But as you know, this delays our market-ready date. When can you guarantee delivery?

SUPPLIER: The 31st.

ACCOUNT: I've got to talk to a few people and see what I can work out. I'll get back to you.

Cooperative–Problem-Solving negotiators (or "Cooperators") are win-win participants who attempt to maximize the return received by both sides in a negotiation. Instead of asking themselves how much of the pie they got, Cooperators realize the importance of asking themselves whether they like what they received. Take the situation above. Both supplier and account fully disclose their concerns and attempt to resolve the problem together. This is a good example of Cooperators conducting themselves in an open, trusting, and objective negotiating manner.

If you are negotiating with a Cooperator, you can expect your counterpart to:

- Begin with realistic opening positions.
- Try to maximize the disclosure of information.
- Rely on objective criteria to guide the discussions and seek to reason with you.
- Rarely resort to threats.
- Seek to maximize the joint returns of both parties.

Cooperators feel most comfortable when they interact with other Cooperatives, and when interactions are congenial. However, Cooperators often leave themselves open to being exploited. If Cooperators behave in their usually open and cooperative manner with Adversaries, they'll fare poorly in negotiations. They give adversarial opponents an edge due to the fact that they disclose more salient information than do manipulative adversaries. If I let a competitive bargaining counterpart know the state of my personal bank account, or what my other options are, he or she will use it to gain leverage during negotiations. To avoid such exploitation, proficient Cooperators behave more competitively when they confront Adversaries. How? By being less generous in both the disclosing of critical information and the making of unreciprocated concessions. This defensive approach enables Cooperators to neutralize the aggressive techniques Adversaries employ against them.

COMPETITIVE–PROBLEM-SOLVING STYLE

There is a huge disadvantage to using the Adversary and Cooperator styles as your only negotiating patterns. That's why the most proficient negotiators use the hybrid Competitiv–Problem-Solving style (or "Innovator") as their primary style. Rich in the flexibility it affords negotiators, the Innovator style, which includes elements of both the Adversary and Cooperator styles where needed, is the most effective strategic method for dealing with different types of negotiators. Here's an example:

SUPERVISOR: New management just reviewed all company employee salaries—most of which have been frozen for three years—with the goal of improving them. We will be making across-the-board salary increases. I can offer you a 20-percent increase in your salary.

SUBORDINATE: I do appreciate that raise, and frankly I'm glad that management is thinking about all the employees. I don't think the 20-percent raise takes into account my added job responsibilities, since the scope of my position has increased by 40 percent during the last year.

SUPERVISOR: I don't have enough money in the budget for such an increase this year, but I will see what I can do about raising your salary commensurate with all your new responsibilities for next year. For now, I think I might be able to give you a 25-percent increase, plus a better title and some stock.

SUBORDINATE: That would be acceptable.

When you negotiate as an Innovator, you will:

- Begin with a strategic opening position, a principled offer that sets the tone for the discussion, using a number of techniques that I will teach you in later chapters of this book.
- Match your counterpart's style on what and how much information you will disclose.
- Rely on objective criteria to guide the discussions, and seek to reason with your counterpart.
- Try to obtain highly beneficial results for yourself, while at the same time striving to maximize *opponent* return, whenever possible.

Which Styles Are Most Effective?

Professor Gerald Williams of Brigham Young University has carefully explored the different negotiating styles of practicing lawyers.[1] He has found that approximately two-thirds of attorneys are considered by their peers to be Cooperators, one-quarter are described as Adversaries, and the remaining individuals are viewed as difficult to classify. These findings are surprising when one considers the inherently competitive traits attributed to most attorneys. Similar findings are obtained with respect to people who negotiate in the business world.

Professor Williams asked the individuals responding to his survey to indicate which lawyers they considered to be proficient negotiators, average negotiators, or ineffective negotiators. While 59 percent of Cooperators were considered effective bargainers, only 25 percent of Adversarial negotiators were considered proficient. His findings with respect to less capable negotiators were even more striking. While only 3 percent of Cooperators were characterized as ineffective, 33 percent of Adversaries were given this low rating. In a more recent study of a similar nature, Professor Andrea Schneider found that over half of Adversaries are now considered ineffective negotiators by their peers.[2]

Many people picture aggressive, tough, and even abrasive people who seek to destroy their opponents by any means available to achieve their goals (adversarial style) as the most successful negotiators. When we contemplate this image from a detached perspective, however, we can appreciate how incorrect this picture is. If someone were to come to your home or workplace to negotiate, announced with overt behavior that he or she planned to clean you out, and exacerbated the situation with gratuitous insults, would you roll over and give the person everything he or she demanded? You would be likely to counter this overtly competitive style with competitive behavior of your own to avoid exploitation. This explains why Cooperators behave more competitively when they encounter openly competitive Adversaries. They begin with less generous opening offers, are less forthcoming with critical information, and try to avoid unreciprocated concessions. In short, they neutralize the competitive conduct of Adversarial opponents.

Adversarial negotiators do *not* obtain more beneficial results than Cooperators. In fact, overtly adversarial bargainers are likely to obtain worse results. Their aggressive behavior discourages many opponents and often leads to non-settlement in situations in which mutually beneficial agreements could otherwise have been achieved. In addition, their competitive conduct reduces the opportunity for cooperative bargaining that would ensure an optimal distribution of the items being exchanged, leading to inefficient agreements.

In the many years I have practiced law and taught negotiating skills, I have not found Cooperators any less effective than Adversaries. The idea that people must be uncooperative, selfish, manipulative, and even abrasive to obtain beneficial results is clearly incorrect. To achieve good bargaining terms, individuals simply have to possess the ability to say "no" forcefully and believably. They can do this courteously and quietly, and be as effective as those who do so more demonstrably. This is why Innovators who use the best characteristics of Cooperators and Adversaries tend to be successful.

What Successful Negotiators Do

Proficient negotiators try to obtain beneficial results for themselves, but seek to accomplish this in a congenial manner. Whatever their philosophy or approach, Intelligent Negotiators prepare thoroughly by taking the following steps:

1. *Know yourself:* Know your bottom line and what your goals are.

2. *Know your counterpart:* Research your counterpart's resources, motivations, and situations well enough to estimate his or her bottom line and aspirations.

Skilled bargainers then use this information to maximize their return, but also strive to maximize opponent return, when this can be accomplished at minimal cost to themselves. Why?

1. They need to satisfy their bargaining counterparts' interests sufficiently to induce them to enter agreements.

2. They know that other parties may experience buyer's remorse and try to back out of the deal if they ultimately regret the terms.

3. They recognize that they will often have future dealings with their present bargaining counterparts.

People who think they were treated poorly are likely to seek revenge in future encounters with those who treated them unfavorably. On the other hand, negotiators who feel they were given fair deals are likely to be more generous in future dealings with those they remember favorably.

What Successful Negotiators Never Do

The best negotiators never take the process personally. They appreciate the fact that their counterparts are merely trying to get good results for themselves and are not intentionally attempting to hurt them. A good negotiator interprets a comment such as "That is an insultingly low offer" as a judgment on the offer, not on the person who made it. It is difficult to maintain this attitude when a prospective house buyer elaborates on design flaws of the home you've lived in for ten years, but a good negotiator remembers that assessing the value of items to be exchanged is part of the bargaining process.

Whenever you bargain, always keep the relationship in view. The other side is *not* the enemy. The person may in fact be someone you respect, admire, or care deeply about. He or she simply has something you want to obtain, or wants something you possess. If you can effectively enhance your bargaining encounters through more courteous behavior, you will enjoy the process more and increase the probability of successful interactions.

As Felicia Brown (whom you met in the introduction) begins her search for a new position, she wants to be an Innovator. She hopes to gain new employment with favorable terms, but recognizes the need to provide her new employer with a fair return on its investment. If she behaves too competitively when she negotiates her initial employment terms, she may either lose the offer or begin her new relationship on a sour note. On the other hand, if she fails to appreciate the fact that business firms expect her to bargain over her new conditions of employment and is hesitant to ask for more beneficial terms, she will short-change herself and jeopardize her future job satisfaction with that company.

A Note about Ethnic and Gender Differences

When we negotiate with others, we initially feel most comfortable with people who are similar to us in terms of age, ethnicity, gender, religion, and socio-economic status. Similarity induces trust and reduces the need for the participants to maintain a particular "face" in each other's eyes. When we interact with individuals who are different from us in these regards, we often distract ourselves by trying to verify the positive and negative images we may have of people similar to those with whom we are conversing. Such stereotypical assumptions can wreak havoc with encounters. By being aware of the human tendency to stereotype, you can lessen its impact on your negotiations.

Ethnicity

When African-Americans, Asian-Americans, European-Americans, and Latino-Americans interact, they are preliminarily influenced by stereotypical beliefs that members of each group have regarding members of other groups and of their own group. Many of my law students—regardless of their ethnicity—think that European-Americans (particularly males) are the most Machiavellian and competitive negotiators. They expect them to use the manipulative adversarial style, looking only to generate optimal results for themselves. On the other hand, students expect African-American, Asian-American, and Latino-American negotiators to use a more cooperative style, assuming them to be desirous of win-win results. When counterparts fail to conform to these stereotyped perceptions, the bargaining process often gets derailed.

Establish trusting and cooperative relationships with counterparts of different ethnic backgrounds before you engage in serious substantive discussions. Never assume that members of particular ethnic groups will be more or less competent, more or less cooperative or competitive, or more or less pleasant to deal with. Each individual must be evaluated to determine his or her unique personal strengths and weaknesses. If you do not assess your counterpart realistically, your stereotypical beliefs will interfere with your ability to fully interact with that person.

Always acknowledge that the particular personal traits of the individual negotiators determine how each encounter develops. Evaluate and deal with each counterpart differently. Is that person a cooperative, adversarial, or innovative bargainer? Does he or she hold greater, equal, or less bargaining power than you hold concerning the issues on the table? What negotiating techniques do you think can be optimally employed against this negotiator? Try to keep an open mind, and be prepared to respond affirmatively to unanticipated disclosures or changed circumstances.

If you begin a bargaining interaction with the notion that particular counterparts will be less proficient because of their ethnicity or gender, you give your counterparts an inherent advantage. For you have let your guard down and presented them with the opportunity to exploit the situation. If you are the target of such stereotyping by counterparts, take advantage of the situation, and claim everything you can for yourself.

I am occasionally asked whether minority students perform as well on my negotiation exercises as nonminority students. In a recent article, James Sammataro noted the reluctance of African-American athletes to hire African-American agents, apparently believing that European-American agents would obtain better results from white owners.[3] This article induced me to review my own course data to see whether this supposition was correct. I found absolutely no difference between the results achieved by African-American and European-American students in my course.[4] Assuming differences based on the ethnicity of your counterparts can prevent you from successfully negotiating with them.

Gender

Gender-based stereotypes often cause negotiators difficulty when they interact with people of the opposite sex. Men see overt aggressiveness that they consider appropriate when employed by men as inappropriate when used by women. Some female negotiators try to obtain a psychological advantage against male counterparts by, for instance, resorting to foul language and loud voices. Male bargainers who would directly counter these tactics when used by other men find it difficult to respond in kind against "ladies." When male negotiators limit their use of bargaining tactics this way, they provide female bargainers with a great advantage. Conversely, some male negotiators try to obtain a psychological advantage against aggressive female counterparts by questioning their femininity. They hope to embarrass their counterparts and make them feel self-conscious.

Never allow male or female counterparts to undermine your negotiating approach. Any negotiator has the right to use techniques you consider appropriate—regardless of the gender-based stereotypes they may contradict.

If you are a woman and find that the gender-based beliefs of your coworkers are negatively influencing your bargaining interactions, you can raise the subject directly. Politely ask your colleagues if they find it difficult to negotiate with women. They will undoubtedly deny any such problems, but will privately reevaluate their own behavior.

Empirical studies have shown that men and women do not behave identically in competitive situations.[5] Women tend to be initially more trusting and more trustworthy than men, but less willing to forgive violations of their trust. If you are a male negotiator interacting with female counterparts, establish a trusting environment that facilitates the discussions—and be careful not to engage in disingenuous behavior that may destroy the trust that develops. If you are a female negotiator interacting with male counterparts, do not automatically assume you are facing an Adversary; and conversely, male negotiators should not assume female counterparts are Cooperators.

Other gender-based stereotypes may influence male and female bargaining interactions. Men are expected to be task-oriented, while women are supposed to be more concerned with maintaining good relationships. Men are expected to be aggressive and openly competitive, while women are expected to be passive and submissive. When men and women interact, men tend to speak for longer periods of time, and they tend to interrupt more often. In negotiating settings, men tend to use more forceful language, whereas women use more modifiers, such as "don't you think . . ." and "it seems to me . . . ," which undermine their persuasiveness. On the other hand, women are generally better listeners than men, and better readers of nonverbal signals.

When women enter the marketplace, others may work harder to take advantage of them than they would with respect to males. A classic study was conducted by Professor Ian Ayres of car prices offered to men and women by car dealers under identical circumstances.[6] Ayres found that salespeople offer male buyers better deals than female buyers—a difference of several hundred dollars. It is not clear whether sales personnel simply think that women buyers are less capable negotiators or whether they are afraid of being embarrassed by giving overly generous terms to women. This market bias has convinced a number of my former female students to take male friends with them when they purchase new cars. They know it gives them more leverage in this particular bargaining situation.

Do gender-based differences affect results achieved by men and women on identical negotiation exercises? In a recent study, I found support for the theory that women feel less comfortable with overt competition—more women (38.8%) take my Legal Negotiating course on a pass/fail basis than men (26.7%).[7] On the other hand, I found no statistically significant differences in the results achieved by men and women on my negotiation exercises.

If you are a man (or a woman) who stereotypes women as less-proficient bargainers, you provide your female counterparts with a great advantage. Nothing is better than opponents who underestimate your bargaining capabilities. If you are a woman who is taken lightly by male counterparts, do not hesitate to recalibrate your bargaining strategy accordingly. Subtly induce them to give you the information you need to obtain optimal results for yourself.

SUMMARY POINTS

Don't always use a single negotiating strategy.

- The Competitive-Adversarial negotiating style may be most appropriate for impersonal, one-time negotiations. Competitive-Adversarials open bargaining with low offers and high demands, focus principally on their own stated positions rather than reason out solutions, make minimal concessions, and seek to maximize their own returns.

- The Cooperative–Problem-Solver negotiating style is most appropriate for negotiations within ongoing relationships. Cooperative Problem Solvers begin with realistic opening positions, maximize the disclosure of information, rely on objective criteria to guide the discussions, and seek to maximize *joint* party returns.

- The Competitive–Problem-Solver negotiating style, which is characterized by flexibility, is the most effective strategy for dealing with all types. Competitive Problem Solvers begin with strategic opening positions that are principled and designed to set the tone for the discussions, match their counterpart's style of information disclosure, avoid unreciprocated concessions, rely on objective criteria to guide the discussions, and seek to obtain optimal results for themselves while maximizing the joint returns achieved by both sides.

- Assess every bargaining counterpart on his or her own merits; stereotyping counterparts because of gender or ethnicity will hamper the negotiation as well as provide the stereotyped bargainer with a considerable advantage.

Chapter 2

Preparing to Negotiate

Most of us have heard the story of the New York City resident stopped on the street by a visitor who asks, "How do I get to Carnegie Hall?" The New Yorker replies, "Practice, practice, practice!" This adage is as true for negotiators hoping to achieve beneficial bargaining results as for anyone who hopes to perform at Carnegie Hall. Bargaining is a performance, and a highly interactive one at that. The Intelligent Negotiator knows this and prepares thoroughly.

In the bargaining context, knowledge constitutes power. You will attain better results if you come to the bargaining table with as much information as possible. If you appreciate the real value of the items being exchanged, and have a good idea what other options are available to you if you do not reach an agreement with your counterparts, you will have a personal self-assurance guaranteed to undermine the confidence of anyone at the table who is less prepared.

> To locate available positions for network managers in small retail firms in the Metropolis area, Felicia contacted the State University Placement Office and visited several Internet sites that list such openings (such as www.monster.com). She is deliberately looking for a position with a small, established retail company for two reasons. First, she feels comfortable assuming the responsibility for such a firm's computer network, based on her education and experience. Second, while Felicia would like to move into the more lucrative private sector and gain new high-tech experience, she would like a position that has fairly regular hours and would not require extensive night and weekend work.
>
> From her inquiries, Felicia has found three suitable openings. How should she optimize her chances of getting interviews? She fears that most commercial companies would not respect her teaching background, although she considers this experience a plus. She prepared a professional resume that lists her educational and employment background. She described her recent computer science teaching and emphasized her ability to explain technical computer concepts to non-technical people. She is certain this will appeal to company officials who know that their network manager must be able to interact effectively with salespeople, warehouse employees, and advertising personnel. She also noted her work in her school district's computer network.
>
> Felicia's approach has worked well; she has been contacted by two firms and has arranged interviews, one on Tuesday afternoon, the other Wednesday morning. She

plans to take extra resumes with her in case the people interviewing her don't have copies of the one she sent the firms. She is prepared to detail her knowledge of computer networks, and her ability to convey technical information in understandable terms. From job listings on the Internet, she knows that small retail firm network manager positions pay in the $55,000 to $70,000 range. While she doesn't have any private sector network experience, she did help to prepare her high school's advanced homepage and created a school network that allows her and her teaching colleagues to put their course materials and class assignments online.

If Felicia is asked about her present $42,000 salary, she plans to note two critical factors. She only works nine months per year and is contemplating a career change because of the low salaries paid to school teachers. If her $42,000 salary were calculated on a twelve-month basis, it would rise by one-third to $56,000. Since she still enjoys teaching, she would only accept a new position paying at least $60,000.

WHAT WILL BE ON THE TABLE?

One of the initial steps in preparing for a negotiation is to determine the items that may be exchanged. What are you willing to trade? Keep in mind that the most important goal during this step is to expand your bargaining options and bargaining power as much as possible, and to do so while maximizing the potential joint return of both participants. You can identify these items by asking yourself two questions:

1. Which items in your possession does your counterpart want?
2. What does your counterpart have that you wish to get?

Compile a list, putting as many items on the table as possible. The greater the number of items to be exchanged, the stronger the possibility for cooperative bargaining. When only one or two items may be exchanged, the encounter becomes more competitive, as "I want/They want" thinking takes hold, making it more difficult to generate mutually beneficial trades.

Remember, bargaining items do not have to be only tangible goods with objective values; intangible items may also be relevant. For example, if you are trying to resolve a dispute with a neighbor who has demonstrated that the beautiful fruit tree you chopped down was on his side of the property line, it won't be enough simply to offer a replacement tree. An apology will be necessary as well. If you do not offer such an apology, no amount of replacement trees will be considered adequate.

Perhaps in your attempts to negotiate a lower price for a house you are thinking of buying, you criticize the size of the dining room, the absence of a fireplace in the family room, or the color of the exterior walls. These comments may offend the sellers, causing them to withdraw from the discussions even though this limits their selling opportunities. In cases such as this, it is more appropriate for you to take a self-deprecating approach. Praise the aspects of the house you do like, but indicate your financial limitations. This may generate sufficient sympathy to induce the sellers to consider a reduced price. Most people would prefer to sell their house to someone who loves it for a lower price than to someone who has criticized their home for a higher price.

Prioritize Bargaining Items

Next, determine your bargaining priorities. These objectives can be divided into four broad categories:

1. **"Essential" items** include those that you *must obtain* to satisfy your fundamental interests. If these key terms are not resolved to your satisfaction, you would prefer your non-settlement alternatives.

2. **"Important" items** are those that you would very much *like to obtain*, but which you would forego if the "essential" terms were resolved favorably.

3. **"Desirable" items** are those of secondary value that you would be pleased to have, but which you would be willing to exchange for "essential" or "important" terms.

4. **"Indifferent" items** are those you would be perfectly willing to concede to achieve your other bargaining objectives.

Consider Substitutes

When you initially determine the value of particular items, contemplate substitute terms you might accept if you cannot obtain what you want. For example, when buying a new car, you might agree to a higher price if the dealer includes "free" service for the first two years or an extended five-year warranty. Someone shopping for a new outfit might pay more if the salesperson throws in a lovely scarf or a tie. These are win-win exchanges, because the buyer values the additional items at their retail price while the seller values them at their wholesale cost. By sharing the difference between the retail and wholesale values, the transacting parties can agree upon mutually acceptable terms.

Similar trades can be made with respect to less tangible terms. If a new employee is given an exalted title, he or she may agree to a lower salary or a more modest office. Someone else negotiating a new job may focus almost entirely on the salary being offered. If the prospective employer offers $5,000 less than the employee believes she deserves, she may reject the deal. If she doesn't think she can obtain a higher salary level, she should consider indirect forms of compensation. Perhaps the firm would agree to provide her with a company car she could use for personal travel or with valuable training opportunities that would enhance her future employment opportunities. These non-taxable fringe benefits may actually be worth more than the extra $5,000 in salary she was seeking.

Add Extras

Good negotiators recognize that we can rarely get everything we ask for. We also may have to forego some important or desirable items to obtain our essential demands. The Intelligent Negotiator increases the likelihood of achieving his or her critical objectives by expanding the issues being negotiated. If you merely ask for two or three items, you are unlikely to get all those terms. However, if you include several "extra" items, you give yourself some bargaining room.

A friend once told me she was preparing for an important negotiation with her manager. She said that she especially wanted two things—a better office and an elevated job title—but thought he would not agree to both. I asked her what else she could realistically request that her manager would be unwilling to grant. She thought for a minute, and came up with a specific request: a 10-percent pay increase. I suggested that she include this monetary item with her other requests, to give her something to exchange for the two things she really wanted. When she finally met with her manager, he was relieved to give her the two terms she preferred—once she retreated with respect to the pay raise he did not wish to grant! Once she demonstrated her competence in the higher position, she did obtain a modest salary increase.

FORMULATE ARGUMENTS
TO SUPPORT YOUR POSITIONS

Once you have a firm sense of what items are to be negotiated and have the largest possible number of items on that list, prepare cogent arguments to support each one. (That's right, each and every one!) Negotiators who provide persuasive arguments to support the issues they want resolved in a certain way are always more likely to prevail. In addition, if you do this, you will exude a quiet confidence in your own positions that will cause less prepared counterparts to doubt the validity of their own positions.

When you prepare arguments for the items you want, it is imperative that you try to anticipate the arguments your opponents are likely to make. This is true for two reasons: You are unlikely to have your confidence undermined when confronted by claims that you anticipate. In addition, if you accurately predict the arguments your counterparts will advance, you can prepare effective counter-arguments against them.

In commercial negotiations, it is especially helpful to obtain a thorough understanding of the value of the items to be discussed. You may have to do some preliminary comparison shopping to ascertain the typical price range for particular goods or models. For many items, such as cars or services, a perusal of appropriate newspaper or trade journal advertisements may provide sufficient information. Internet shopping services can also be quite useful.

When you are negotiating employment terms, research critical information regarding the compensation plans of your target organization. Seek not only salary data but also fringe benefit packages. On occasion you might find some public information about comparative compensation programs within a field or profession. However, in most cases involving private firms, public salary information is rarely available. Industry studies or friends employed by other companies within the same industry may be able to provide useful figures. If you know people working at the specific firm involved, asking them to provide relevant information is reasonable, as long as you agree not to disclose your source.

The Intelligent Negotiator formulates proposals that are beneficial to both sides. So after you have formulated arguments in support of your positions, develop an understanding of your bargaining counterparts' needs and interests. What are the factors that will induce your counterparts to give you what you hope to achieve? If sales of commercial items are down, retailers may be anxious to make quick sales. If it is near the end of the month or the model year, car dealers may have corporate rebates and corporate incentives encouraging fast deals. How long have particular houses been on the market? The longer they have been available, the more likely it is that sellers have begun to lower their sights in an effort to get on with their lives. Have the sellers already purchased another home elsewhere, generating great financial pressure to take this house off their hands?

When you negotiate with family members, friends, or professional colleagues, intangible interests are often more important than tangible terms. Fairness is one such intangible item. For example, if you got to select last year's vacation destination, deferring to your spouse's desires with respect to this year's choice may be the fair thing to do. Another kind of intangible interest is respect. If you are a supervisor negotiating with subordinates, try to avoid embarrassing your subordinates in front of their peers. In some instances, this may necessitate a thorough discussion of the underlying issues only *after* the subordinates have been separated from their coworkers. If the subordinates appreciate your willingness to postpone the talks until they can be conducted away from other employees, they are more likely to consider your viewpoint. If, on the other hand, you fail to wait for a propitious time and you directly challenge a subordinate in front of his or her colleagues, an unpleasant reaction may result in a needless escalation of the controversy.

Similar considerations apply to bargaining encounters with business partners. If certain proposals are likely to embarrass or anger your partners, soften those proposals when possible. Seemingly equivalent concessions may be offered to minimize the negative impact of unpleasant discussions. Never permit your short-term interests to adversely affect your longer-term relationships, whether business or personal.

Felicia thought her two interviews went well and is pleased when she gets a call from the vice president of Andersen, the company she prefers, offering her a job. Andersen is a three-year-old retail establishment that has been selling high-tech gadgets through four retail locations and mail-order catalogs. Last year, Andersen began to expand its e-commerce and has generated increased Internet sales through its Web site. It needs a network manager who can advance its e-business capabilities. She has to meet tomorrow afternoon with the vice president to discuss the terms of her employment. The original position announcement described the basic employment conditions: a salary of "up to $60,000," employer-paid health coverage, two weeks vacation per year, and a defined-contribution pension plan to which the firm contributes 8 percent of employee compensation.

From a friend at a similar company, Felicia has learned that most network managers at such firms earn from $58,000 to $70,000. Three to four weeks vacation is common, with pension contributions ranging from 7 to 10 percent. A few businesses have bonus programs, with bonus payments of $5,000 to $10,000 for exemplary employees during profitable years. Some have stock option plans that enable employees to purchase company stock at favorable prices. Several provide workers with company cars.

Salary is important to Felicia. She hopes to get $60,000 to $65,000. She plans to mention a $70,000 figure to the vice president to sensitize him to a number in the mid-$60,000 area. If she is unable to get $64,000 or $65,000, she plans to ask whether she could earn a several thousand dollar bonus for good performance. She will also ask whether the firm would consider a raise within six months if her work is excellent.

Felicia plans to ask for four weeks of vacation, hoping to get Andersen to offer at least three weeks. The 8 percent Andersen pension contribution seems fine, and she doesn't need a company car. If necessary, however, she may mention the fact that several similar firms supply network managers with cars in an effort to obtain a higher starting salary or an extra week of vacation.

Although Felicia has a graduate degree in computer science, she wants to take several week-long training programs that pertain to specific software applications. Because these courses would enhance her value to the firm, she wants Andersen to pay for these classes and give her the time off. She also plans to ask the company to pay her dues in several professional associations. Since Bill's agency would pay for most of their moving expenses, Felicia plans to use this item as a bargaining chip to obtain other benefits. She will mention the $5,000 they expect to incur in moving expenses, and agree to forego moving expense reimbursement if she can obtain permission to attend company-paid training programs and get the firm to pay her association dues.

WHAT'S YOUR BOTTOM LINE?

Your next step is to evaluate your non-settlement options or, in other words, the best arrangements you could obtain for yourself if you were unable to reach any agreement in your upcoming bargaining sessions. Roger Fisher and William Ury, in their classic negotiating guide *Getting to Yes*, described this point by the term BATNA—your Best Alternative to a Negotiated Agreement.[1] The Intelligent Negotiator uses BATNA as his or her *bottom line.* Refuse to enter into a negotiated deal that is worse than the circumstances you would have without any accord. Never go below your bottom line.

What Non-Settlement Options Are Available to You?

Examine your non-settlement options, such as these: Ask yourself how much do you want the terms you hope to obtain from the other side? What alternatives can you live with if no present accord is achieved? How satisfactory would these alternatives be in comparison to what this opponent could provide?

For instance, you want a promotion, a higher salary, and better long-term career opportunities than your present situation allows. And you've just been offered a job at a competitive company in another city. Are you willing to relocate to obtain a preferable position? Would you be willing to consider a different industry or an entirely different occupation if you could stay where you are and receive better long-term opportunities than you now have? Are you willing to return to school full- or part-time to obtain the skills you need to enter new occupations? What other firms could offer you suitable employment? Could you seek a transfer to another position within your present company that might preclude your need to look elsewhere?

By diligently searching for acceptable non-settlement options, you can enhance your bargaining power with respect to your present adversaries. The better the external alternatives you develop for yourself, the greater the bargaining freedom you will possess when you are in the thick of the bargaining encounter.

What Non-Settlement Options Are Available to Your Opponent?

Once you have developed an appreciation of the different settlement and non-settlement options available to you, and have identified your bottom line, try to place yourself in the shoes of your *counterpart*. Ask yourself what options would be available to the other side if it failed to reach a deal with you. Many negotiators fail to evaluate the options available to their opponents. This is a critical oversight, for your bargaining power is determined by these factors. Comparing your bottom line with your opponent's bottom line is the best way to measure bargaining power. If your non-settlement options are better than those of your adversary, you have greater bargaining power—and vice-versa.

Several years ago, a close friend told me about a significant corporate dispute in which he was involved. He explained the factual circumstances and acrimonious bargaining history, and said he was beside himself and didn't know how to proceed. I asked what would happen to his firm if no agreement were achieved. He replied that they would be bankrupt. When I asked how bad that would be, he was shocked. I asked whether his company could go through bankruptcy reorganization, and he said they

TIP

When Intelligent Negotiators measure their own bottom line against those of their counterparts, they often undervalue their own options and overvalue those of the other side. It is human nature to become intimately familiar with our own circumstances. We often dwell on the negative aspects of our situations, assuming our counterparts are aware of those matters. When we are upset, we even magnify the negative factors that affect us. When we attempt to evaluate our opponents' circumstances, however, we tend to do the opposite. We see the strengths the other side possesses, and often miss the negative pressures affecting that party. When you evaluate the circumstances affecting the other side, try to look behind the facade being projected and speculate about the problems likely to be influencing that side. What hidden pressures may be driving the other party? How much does that side need what you can provide?

No matter what the balance of power, Intelligent Negotiators project their strengths and conceal their weaknesses. What you must ask yourself when preparing for bargaining is not what weaknesses you actually possess, but what weaknesses you have that your opponent is likely to recognize. Think about the impression the other side has of your situation. If you do a good job of hiding your problem areas, you should be able to create an image of greater strength.

could. I then asked what would happen to the opposing corporation if no agreement were achieved. He said he had no idea. When I urged him to think about this carefully, he indicated that they would also be bankrupt. I asked whether they could reorganize, and he replied negatively. His firm was the other company's main client, and if their relationship was severed, the other corporation would be out of business. My friend finally appreciated the bargaining advantage he possessed, by virtue of the fact that his non-settlement alternative, while not pleasant, was substantially preferable to the negative impact a non-settlement would have on the opposing party.

When comparing settlement and non-settlement options, always include the transactional costs associated with both alternatives. What are the financial and emotional costs of agreement, and what are the economic and psychological costs associated with no agreement? Even when the monetary transaction costs may be relatively equal, other considerations may lead you to favor a negotiated resolution.

The fact the underlying situation will be resolved now instead of months from now may provide financial and/or emotional relief. On the other hand, a bad settlement is almost always worse than a preferable non-settlement, because of the post-settlement "buyer's remorse" experienced by those of us who consent in haste to poor agreements.

Felicia Brown realizes that present employment market considerations enhance her bargaining position. Unemployment in the Metropolis area is low, and businesses are finding it hard to attract skilled workers. She thus thinks she can get at least $60,000 elsewhere if she rejects the Andersen offer, and has decided not to accept an Andersen salary below $62,000 or $63,000. By examining job announcements for similar firms, Felicia believes she should be able to get Andersen to cover the cost of at least some of her training programs and agree to three weeks of vacation.

Felicia is aware of the number of network manager positions available, and appreciates the difficulty Andersen would have finding a proficient person if she turns them down. Even though she does not want to apply for many of these vacant positions, due to the extended hours and high stress situations involved, she knows that Andersen has to compete for people who might be willing to work for larger firms if the employment terms were sufficiently generous. Felicia thus appreciates the fact that Andersen probably needs her services more than she needs their job.

Establish Firm and Appropriate Aspiration Levels: Those Who Want Better Deals, Get Better Deals

By now you know your bottom line and your non-settlement options, as well as those of your opponents. It is time to establish your aspiration level. Begin the process by asking yourself: What do I hope to achieve through this bargaining encounter? How well can I possibly hope to do?

As stated above, *Persons who want better deals get better deals.* So set your goals high. If you think in terms of your bottom line, you are unlikely to obtain terms any more generous than that initial level. When in doubt, raise your goals. If your new objectives seem unattainable, take the time to develop arguments supporting them. Do not open discussions until you feel personally comfortable with your elevated objectives. This will enable you to exude an inner confidence that undermines a less prepared opponent's belief in his or her own position.

When I teach negotiation courses, I regularly notice the same phenomenon. Individuals who begin a bargaining encounter with lower expectations achieve their reduced objectives and are pleased with their results—until I announce the terms attained by other negotiators who had set higher goals. On the other hand, people who begin an interaction with elevated goals may be unable to obtain everything they want, causing them to doubt the degree of success they have achieved. Only after the group results are disclosed do these people appreciate how well they have done. The irony of this situation is the fact that people who always set minimal goals get those terms and are more pleased with their results than are more adroit colleagues who establish higher objectives but fall slightly short of their targets.

If you always or almost always get what you initially hope to achieve when you enter bargaining interactions, you should begin to raise your aspiration levels, initially, by 10 to 15 percent. If you try to double or triple your planned goals, you are likely to fail and return to your old tendencies. If you continue to get everything you seek, raise your objectives again in 10 to 15 percent increments until you begin to occasionally fall short of your targets. At this point, you can be confident that you have learned to establish appropriately elevated aspiration levels.

Almost every year, a third-year law student comes to my office to discuss an impending negotiation. The student has received an employment offer from a smaller law firm that does not have a definite compensation policy. The partner has merely indicated that the firm has "competitive salaries." The student is scheduled to have lunch the next day with the hiring partner to discuss the salary to be paid. My conversation with these students is almost always the same:

PROFESSOR CRAVER: Have you asked classmates who have received offers from comparable firms what salaries they have received?

STUDENT: Yes. One is getting $80,000, another $78,000, a third $73,000, and a fourth $69,000.

PROFESSOR CRAVER: When the partner asks you if you know what similar firms are paying new associate attorneys, casually mention the $80,000 and $78,000 figures and become silent. Look at the partner with confident anticipation.

STUDENT: Should I mention the lower salaries paid by the other two firms?

PROFESSOR CRAVER: No. Wait and see whether the partner wishes to do so. Most firms don't like to admit that they are not comparable to the higher paying firms, thus there is a good chance the partner will not discuss the other two firms.

What is the minimum salary you hope to obtain?

STUDENT: I would really like to get at least $70,000 to $72,000, if possible.

PROFESSOR CRAVER: You should be able to get the $80,000 being paid by the first firm you mentioned.

STUDENT: I couldn't possibly do that well!

PROFESSOR CRAVER: If a classmate was able to get that salary at a similar firm, you should be able to do so. Try to enjoy your lunch tomorrow. I know you are going to do well.

The student begins to contemplate the $80,000 figure and departs. Several days later, he returns to my office looking somewhat dejected.

PROFESSOR CRAVER: How did your meeting with the hiring partner go?

STUDENT: Not so well. I only got $78,000.

PROFESSOR CRAVER: That's great! I didn't think you would do that well.

STUDENT: I don't understand. You said I should be able to get $80,000, and I only got $78,000.

PROFESSOR CRAVER: You had to think $80,000 to get the $78,000. If you had gone to lunch hoping to get only $70,000 to $72,000, you would probably have accepted $70,000—and possibly even $68,000.

Only at this point does the student begin to appreciate the importance of a high and firm aspiration level. Had the student not expected to obtain the $80,000 salary, he could not have hoped to get the $78,000 figure achieved. The student might even have gone below his initial $70,000 to $72,000 goal.

When multiple item negotiations are involved, an Intelligent Negotiator establishes specific aspirations for *each* of the items being exchanged. If you only create overall aspirations or provide goals for some items, when you get to terms for which you have no real objectives, you are likely to cave. You have not developed set reference points for these items, thus you have no touchstones to guide your actions when they address them. Adroit adversaries can exploit this lack of item-specific preparation by seizing these terms after the other issues have been resolved.

As she prepares for her meeting with the Andersen vice-president, Felicia's confidence level begins to rise. She initially hoped to get at least $60,000, but now thinks she may be able to get $63,000 or $64,000. She believes she can definitely obtain three weeks of vacation, and can probably get Andersen to pay for most of her training classes as well as give her the time off to attend those classes. She will try to get either the possibility of an annual performance bonus or the promise of a salary reassessment after her first six months of employment.

Felicia plans to mention her anticipated moving expenses and the possibility of a company car to induce Andersen to make concessions on other items. If they indicate a willingness to give her several thousand dollars in moving expenses, she plans to request a "signing bonus" instead. She knows that Bill's agency would not reimburse him for any moving expenses covered by Andersen, but would make no similar deduction for a signing bonus given to her. Andersen should not mind how such a payment is characterized, since the cost to them would be the same in either case.

PREPARE YOUR OPENING OFFER

Intelligent Negotiators appreciate the importance of opening offers. That's why they plan ahead and use effective bargaining techniques such as the ones discussed below.

Use the Bracketing Phenomenon to Your Advantage

A bargaining phenomenon known as *bracketing* works as follows: Once an offer is made, bargainers tend to move toward the midpoint between their opening positions. Good bargainers try to establish initial offers that, when averaged with the anticipated offers of opponents, will provide the desired objectives. The "bracketing" phenomenon explains why most negotiators prefer to have counterparts announce their beginning positions first. Once your opponents have made an opening offer, you can adjust your initial proposals to keep your goals near the center of your respective opening offers. For example, you hope to obtain $75,000. Your counterpart begins with a $68,000 offer, so you respond with an $82,000 demand. If the parties make equal concessions thereafter, you will achieve your $75,000 objective. If you are making the opening offer: Try to estimate where your opponents will begin the encounter, then select a beginning position that would most likely result in final terms favorable to yourself.

Give Yourself Some Bargaining Room

Many inexperienced negotiators are afraid to offer elevated opening bids that might offend their opponents. As a result, they begin with position statements that are not particularly generous to themselves, and they obtain below average settlement results. This is a mistake. Intelligent Negotiators usually attempt to develop the most extreme opening positions that they can *rationally defend*. Remember that *indefensible* positions will cause an immediate loss of credibility, and appreciate the degree to which you may elevate your claims in a defensible manner if you carefully prepare the arguments necessary to support your proposals. When in doubt, begin with inflated positions that provide you with room for movement once the serious discussions begin.

There are several reasons to start high. It is impossible for anyone, even the most highly skilled bargainers among us, to accurately calculate the true value of impending interactions solely from our own perspective. Until you begin to interact with your counterparts, you have no idea how much they want the prospective deal. You don't know how risk-averse or risk-taking those persons may be. Your counterparts might be risk-averse people who feel compelled to achieve agreements, in which case they may be willing to accept less beneficial terms. On the other hand, if your counterparts are risk-takers who are willing to accept the consequences associated with non-settlements, you may have to moderate your aspirations. Open discussions with a heightened position statement so you can preserve your options until you are able to determine whether your preliminary assessments are accurate.

Consider the Impact of Anchoring

Some of us prefer to begin bargaining encounters with modest proposals in the hope that we will generate reciprocal behavior by our opponents. However, such behavior is likely to have the opposite effect. For example, you go to a car dealer to purchase a new vehicle. If the salesperson begins the serious discussions by emphasizing the $22,500 manufacturer's suggested retail price (MSRP), you may be pleased with a $21,500 deal, elated that you obtained a $1,000 price reduction. On the other hand, if the salesperson begins with the $21,500 figure, you would feel the need to achieve a price below that level. If the salesperson refused to go much below $21,500, you may walk out and try to get a better deal elsewhere. *Anchoring* explains why, when we receive opening offers that are more generous than anticipated, we first question our own preliminary evaluations and then begin to think we will do better than we hoped.

Negotiators who begin with less generous preliminary offers have the opposite anchoring impact. You induce opponents to think they will be unable to do as well as they had anticipated, causing them to lower their expectation levels. This phenomenon increases the probability of final settlements and enhances the likelihood you will achieve beneficial terms for yourself.

Several months ago, I flew back to Reagan National Airport from an out-of-town speaking engagement. I took a taxi home to my Georgetown residence. We don't have metered cabs, but use an incomprehensible zone system to determine taxi fares. The fare for my Reagan National trip home usually costs between $14 and $16, plus tip. On this occasion, the driver demanded $26! I laughed, and said his demand set an all-time record. He then demanded $21. I handed him a $20 bill and suggested he call the police if he expected a higher fare. He accepted my $20 bill and departed. Nonetheless, because of his outrageous opening demand of $26, he got the highest amount I have ever paid for that ride. The "anchoring" effect of his $26 demand made me feel lucky to get out of the cab for only $20. Had he been more honest with his initial demand, he would only have received $16 or $18.

Bear in Mind the Impact of Gain-Loss Framing

Another layer to consider when making your opening bid is *gain-loss framing*. Studies by experts like Daniel Kahneman and Amos Tversky have demonstrated the impact of this phenomenon.[2] People behave differently when considering *sure gains* or *sure losses*. Those deciding whether to accept a certain gain or the possibility of a greater gain or no gain tend to be risk-averse. They usually accept the certain gain. A perfect example is the television show "Who Wants to Be a Millionaire?" When contestants get to the $64,000 or $125,000 level and are contemplating a question at the next higher level, they only provide an answer when they are quite sure it is correct. They would rather keep the certain $64,000 or $125,000 than risk a fall-back to the $32,000 level. On the other hand, people facing a certain loss or the possibility of a greater loss or no loss tend to be risk-takers—hoping to avoid any loss. When you prepare your opening offer, try to frame what you are offering as "gain" for your counterparts, as this will make them more risk-averse. Even when it appears that your opponents must lose money, point out how much they will "gain" by achieving a peaceful resolution of the present conflict. For instance, if an antiques dealer asks $400 for a vintage rocking chair, you should frame your opening offer of $250 as a sure gain (as you have the cash now and have bought similar pieces for less money).

If you do this, the dealer is more likely to see your offer as an opportunity and consider it fully.

Prepare Principled Opening Offers

When adroit negotiators prepare for bargaining interactions, they try to develop principled explanations they can use to support the particular positions they are articulating. For example, instead of simply offering $21,500 for a specific vehicle with certain options, they note the basic dealer cost of $19,000, the $1,000 dealer cost for the luxury package, and the $500 dealer cost for the enhanced sound system. Prospective home-buyers making an initial offer for a house would note the recent selling prices for similar homes in the same geographical area. They would mention the comparable homes that sold for less, rather than the homes that sold for more, leaving it to the selling agent to note the higher priced transactions. If the selling agent fails to point out the higher priced houses, he or she may undermine the chance of obtaining a higher price for this home.

Providing a careful explanation for your initial position accomplishes two objectives: It explains why you are offering your initial terms instead of more generous terms. It also begins to undermine opponents' confidence in their own positions. If your adversaries can be induced to question the propriety of their preliminary evaluations, they are likely to move in your direction.

When negotiating with family members, close friends, or business partners, you will find it difficult to begin with positions as extreme as those you might use with strangers in commercial settings. It still behooves you to begin with offers that provide some bargaining room and that will, through anchoring, moderate the other's expectations. If you start with offers that are overly generous, your spouses, children, friends, or business associates will be likely to raise their expectation levels in a way that will make the attainment of mutually acceptable resolutions more difficult.

> From the position announcement indicating that Andersen planned to pay "up to $60,000" for the network manager position, Felicia anticipates that the vice-president will begin discussions with a $55,000 to $57,000 offer. She wisely recognizes that almost all employers initially offer less than they are willing to pay, hoping to hire new workers for less than necessary. They expect knowledgeable job candidates to make counteroffers, and wish to provide themselves with room to make needed concessions. Job applicants who fail to appreciate this fact and accept the terms initially tendered forego the more beneficial terms they could have obtained through the bargaining process.
>
> Felicia originally planned to ask Andersen for a $65,000 salary, but appreciates the bargaining leverage the tight labor market affords her. If the vice president offers her $55,000, she decides to politely note the $70,000 and more being earned by network managers at firms that are only slightly larger than Andersen. By inducing the Andersen vice president to think in this exalted range, Felicia believes that he would be likely to move quickly to $60,000—and may even contemplate a higher figure. This approach should certainly get Felicia past her $60,000 bottom line, and near her $63,000 to $64,000 target.
>
> Felicia plans to request four weeks vacation, reimbursement for her moving expenses, firm payment for

the training courses she wants to take, a modest "signing bonus," and a company car. She plans to concede the moving expenses and company car quickly, in exchange for the other items she desires more. These concessions would make the vice president feel relieved when he only has to give her the signing bonus and course payments.

CHOREOGRAPHING IMPENDING INTERACTIONS

Plan ahead. Think about how you will induce your opponents to move from their opening positions to where you want them to end up. You want to choreograph the impending interaction in a manner that enhances the probability that you will obtain the terms you wish to get. Following the presentation of opening positions, do you envision a few large concessions or a series of smaller concessions? Which of the different bargaining techniques (featured in chapter 8) do you plan to use to move the opponents in your direction? The more you envision being successful, the more likely you are to achieve your ultimate objectives. Since your adversaries may not behave exactly as you anticipated, you must retain sufficient flexibility to counteract unexpected opponent conduct.

Plan When and Where to Negotiate

Don't be so concerned about the substantive aspects of your upcoming bargaining encounter that you fail to consider the *contextual factors*—the time, date, and setting for the discussions. These essential factors frame the negotiation.

Skilled negotiators sometimes permit the other party to choose the location in order to demonstrate their good faith and to create more cooperative environments. Most people feel more comfortable in familiar surroundings and prefer, whenever possible, to negotiate in their own homes or offices. However, when dealing with retail establishments, the salespeople generally control the negotiating environments. Prospective buyers must normally go to the retail stores, car dealerships, or real estate offices involved.

If the discussions are to occur in a location that you select, how do you plan to arrange the furniture? If there is a square or rectangular table in the room, angry adversaries are likely to take seats on opposite sides of the table. This confrontational configuration heightens the anxiety level and lessens the possibility of a pleasant interaction. If you can select a round or oval table and have the participants sit adjacent to one another around the table, this more cooperative setting should enhance the talks. Even if a square or rectangular table is used, seating the participants on adjacent sides, instead of directly across from one another, can similarly enhance the bargaining environment. If a sofa is available, you can create a cooperative situation by having the parties sit next to one another.

If you go to the other side's office and feel uncomfortable as soon as you enter the negotiating space, look around and ask yourself whether this person has deliberately set the room up to make *you* feel uncomfortable. Has he or she sat in a raised chair and given you a short, uncomfortable chair? Has he or she taken up most of the space with his or her own desk and chair, forcing you to sit in a chair with your back against the wall to place you on the defensive?

Some adversaries may place your chair in a place where you will have bright sunlight in your eyes! A few unscrupulous car dealers or real estate agents place hidden microphones in the room so they can listen to your conversations with your spouse or partner when you think you are conferring confidentially. If you ever encounter such opponents, remember one thing: They are viciously competitive individuals who will do whatever it takes to defeat you. Be on your guard, and don't hesitate to use the "attitudinal bargaining" discussed in chapter 3 to moderate their offensive behavior. If you suspect that your opponents are eavesdropping on your side's private conversations, plan what you will say ahead of time to limit what your adversaries may hear. You can then communicate silently with hand gestures or on paper when necessary to prevent discovery by unscrupulous opponents.

SUMMARY POINTS

Prepare thoroughly for negotiations using the following steps:

- Compile a list of as many as possible items that may be exchanged, and decide which items are "essential," "important," "desirable," and "indifferent."

- Prepare arguments to support the terms you want.

- Determine your bottom line by deciding your best alternative to a negotiated agreement.

- Estimate the best non-settlement options available to your counterparts.

- Establish firm aspiration levels, and set them high. Those who ask for better deals get better deals.

- Prepare the most generous opening offers you can rationally defend, both to give yourself bargaining room and to "anchor" the preliminary discussions close to your end of the settlement range.

- Visualize how you plan to move from where negotiations begin to where you hope they will end up.

- Select an optimal time and location for bargaining encounters.

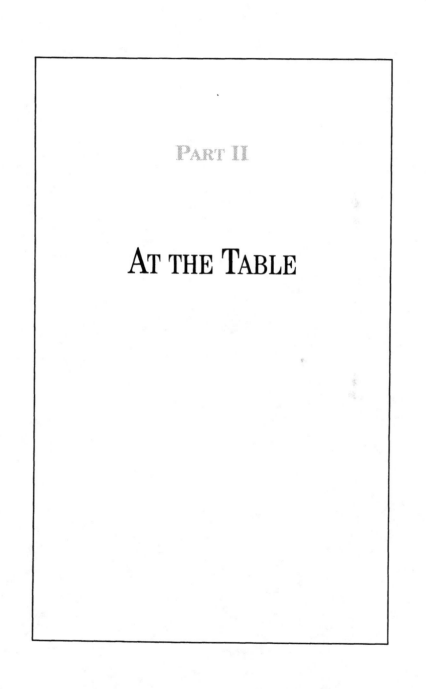

PART II

AT THE TABLE

Chapter 3

Building Rapport and Setting the Tone

Bargaining begins at the point of first contact. An Intelligent Negotiator strives to create, from that first step forward, positive relationships and an optimistic negotiating environment. In this chapter you will learn several ways to create this.

First, assess what you already know about those with whom you will be negotiating. Have you negotiated with these counterparts before? Just once, maybe twice, or perhaps several times? For example, if you are discussing price with a regular supplier of yours, or you and your business partner are divvying up the responsibilities for a new project, you are already familiar with each other's personality and negotiating style. Here you can begin discussions without having to establish new ground rules.

However, if your prior dealings with this counterpart were anything less than extensive—for instance, you're dealing with a new client or recently hired account manager—expect to spend the initial moments of your negotiation establishing some personal rapport and setting the desired tone for the discussions.

If you are not at all familiar with the bargaining styles and philosophies of your counterparts, seek out pre-bargaining information about these people from friends or colleagues who may know them. Try to discover whether your prospective counterparts are cooperative or adversarial, pleasant or unpleasant, honest or less than honest, and realistic or unrealistic. By obtaining such intelligence, you can prepare for the kinds of encounters you may reasonably anticipate.

> Felicia has a friend who knows the Andersen vice president. From him, she has learned that the vice president is a friendly and open person. She hopes they can get on a first-name basis quickly, to personalize their interaction. Since she likes direct people who say what they're thinking without playing games, she thinks she is likely to have a productive and pleasant bargaining encounter with the vice president.

CREATE A POSITIVE NEGOTIATING ENVIRONMENT

No matter how familiar your counterparts are to you, creating a positive atmosphere is always a prerequisite to cooperative, win-win interactions. Begin in-person discussions with warm handshakes and smiles. *Personalize the interaction.* As soon as it is socially acceptable, try to get on a first-name basis to remind your counterpart that you are engaged in personal interactions. (When dealing with individuals from foreign cultures that have more formal social structures, however, be careful not to use first names too quickly in a manner that may offend your counterparts.) By emphasizing the personal nature of your encounters, you will diminish the likelihood of negative behavior that is more likely to occur during impersonal transactions.

You'll most likely begin your exchange with small talk about traffic, the weather, sports, and mutual acquaintances. These comments may continue for only a minute or two, or they may continue for a longer period of time. These ritualistic exchanges are *not* a waste of valuable time, but are in fact quite important. They establish the tone for the subsequent discussions. If you and your counterparts do not begin your substantive talks on a positive note, you are effectively handicapping yourselves.

Although personalizing bargaining encounters is beneficial, it is helpful to *depersonalize* the *conflicts* that you must address. Separate the people from the negative issues. This will allow you to diminish the impact of emotions that do not directly affect the problems on the table. The only exception to this is when you deal with interpersonal conflicts in which personal feelings play an important role. In these situations, acknowledge the emotions that contributed to the conflict, and keep them firmly in mind as you address opposing parties.

Think in terms of the conflict when you are evaluating another bargainer's strategy. Do not take the process personally simply because you know your opponents wish to obtain better terms than they give up. That is a normal aspect of bargaining encounters. After all, you should be trying to get better results for yourself.

Learn from the Innovators' approaches: Be open, flexible. If your opponents seem cooperative, try to verify whether their actual behavior is consistent with their apparent predisposition toward open, win-win interactions. During the initial discussions, carefully watch to see whether your adversaries are providing you with information as valuable as the information you are disclosing. If your openness is not being reciprocated, start behaving more strategically. You need to avoid creating an information imbalance favoring your less-forthcoming opponents. Disclosing too much critical information about your own strengths and weaknesses without obtaining reciprocal disclosures from your opponents leaves you vulnerable to manipulation. If, on the other hand, you decide that your opponents are sincerely cooperating, do all you can to reinforce that behavior since this will encourage more open discussions and minimize the likelihood that your adversaries will resort to inappropriate tactics.

Some individuals exhibit overtly competitive tendencies at the beginning of their bargaining interactions. Their office environments are designed to make their counterparts feel uncomfortable. They have large comfortable chairs for themselves and short uncomfortable chairs for you. Their desk and chair take up much of the office space, while the visitor chairs have their backs near the wall. When such individuals are forced to go to the offices of others, they select seats directly across from, instead of adjacent to, their counterparts. They exude little warmth. They sometimes begin talks with their arms folded across their chests and with their legs crossed in a closed and unreceptive manner. They often address you by your last name, even when you are addressing them by their first names. This permits them to depersonalize their interactions with persons they view as their enemy. They find it easier psychologically to use manipulative tactics against individuals with whom they have not established personal relationships.

The initial portions of bargaining interactions form the framework of the entire encounter. When interactions begin on a hostile or untrusting note, subsequent discussions are likely to be less open and more adversarial than when the discussion began in a congenial and cooperative manner. Even inherently competitive bargaining encounters—such as those involving money—do not have to be conducted in a hostile fashion. In fact, negotiators who can induce their opponents to like them are usually able to obtain better results than bargainers who generate negative reactions.

Skilled negotiators, whichever style they use, recognize that uncivilized conduct undermines the bargaining process. So try to maintain a courteous demeanor. When you encounter rude or nasty behavior, remember that such conduct is a substitute for bargaining proficiency. It is usually employed by less capable negotiators. Never emulate inappropriate behavior. By maintaining a professional approach, you will embarrass rude adversaries and enhance the likelihood of obtaining what you seek. It is always easier to gain concessions from people you are treating well than from individuals you are insulting. Furthermore, if your politeness embarrasses your overly aggressive opponents, they may even make unplanned concessions to assuage their guilty consciences.

When Felicia is ushered into the vice president's office, he greets her warmly and introduces himself as Richie Solomon, making it clear that he expects to be called "Richie." He indicates how pleased Andersen is to offer Felicia the network manager position, and notes her excellent qualifications. He says that he is certain they can agree upon mutually beneficial employment terms. Solomon immediately puts Felicia at ease and induces her to think that everything will be fine.

ATTITUDINAL BARGAINING

When your subtle behavior fails to disarm your overtly competitive or even abrasive counterparts, address the problem more directly through *attitudinal bargaining*. Begin by indicating your unwillingness to view the bargaining process as a competitive, win-lose endeavor and suggesting your desire to establish some preliminary ground rules. If you are seeking to enter into a new business relationship, you can say that you are looking for a mutually beneficial partnership and have no plans to do business with someone who treats you disrespectfully. If you are trying to negotiate with a family member or close friend, you can just ask the other person why he or she has begun the talk in such an inappropriate fashion. Is he or she angry about something you may have done, or upset about something else? If you can disclose and deflect the underlying problem, you can create a more positive negotiating atmosphere.

I remember a discussion with the General Counsel of a large insurance company who told me how amazed he is by the number of claimant lawyers who begin their discussions over large claims with insulting behavior. He simply informs such attorneys that he is the person who decides whether they get any money. He then indicates that if their inappropriate conduct continues, he will not negotiate with them. This attitudinal bargaining usually has the requisite impact, as claimant lawyers who wish to obtain generous settlement terms moderate their behavior.

When you obtain advance intelligence from others indicating that particular counterparts are likely to approach bargaining interactions in an adversarial and even abrasive manner, prepare to counteract this anticipated behavior. If the discussions will take place in your home or office, provide a hospitable negotiating environment and a warm welcome when the talks begin. Although you should be careful not to disclose too much critical information without receiving reciprocal cooperation, your overtly cooperative conduct may induce some competitive negotiators to moderate their behavior. If your preliminary cooperative overtures are not matched, proceed with caution.

> Because of the pleasant way in which Vice President Solomon has begun his discussions with Felicia, she is confident they will have a cooperative and productive interaction. When Solomon takes a seat next to her, instead of returning to the large chair behind his desk, she feels more comfortable. He clearly wants to deal with her on an equal, rather than on a superior-subordinate basis.

Dealing with Obstreperous Counterparts

You may encounter adversarial counterparts whose tactics cannot be moderated through attitudinal bargaining. When this happens, attempt to control the interactions in ways that will diminish the capacity of these aggressors to adversely affect you. For example, when faced with sarcastic and belittling opponents, use the telephone to conduct your talks. When opponents begin to bother you with offensive tactics, you can indicate that you have other calls or other matters to take care of then break off discussions. You can then call such opponents back after you have calmed down. If particularly aggressive opponents try to intimidate you by invading your personal space (for example, sitting too close to you or standing over you) during in-person encounters, you can meet in a conference room or a dining room containing a large table and place your opponents on the opposite side of the table. This makes it difficult for your adversaries to invade your territory, since such behavior would be pathetically obvious and thus ineffective.

When you're engaged in conduct that has offended someone else and you know those people are terribly upset, acknowledge the other side's feelings. Politely permit other parties to express their viewpoint without interruption. Such venting will allow those counterparts to say what they have to say in an environment that should diminish the intensity of the offense. When those persons have finished speaking, indicate that you have heard their message. It can also be helpful, when appropriate, for you to apologize for any conduct that may have contributed to the discomfort of your counterparts. There is no reason for you to accept the blame for circumstances over which you had no control, but suggesting you are sorry for the other person's feelings or for the negative consequences suffered by him or her can effectively contribute to the healing process. Once distraught counterparts feel their emotions have been respected, they can more easily talk objectively about the actions they seek to correct the situation.

SUMMARY POINTS

- Initial contact is the critical point for setting the tone for the entire negotiation.

- Skilled negotiators create positive negotiation environments by personalizing the interaction.

- If you are a Cooperator, be sure your openness is being reciprocated before you disclose too much information and expose yourself to exploitation by Adversaries who are being less forthright.

- Attitudinal bargaining is effective when seeking to establish beneficial ground rules with especially aggressive counterparts.

- When proficient negotiators are unable to eliminate offensive opponent behavior, they try to control the interaction in a way that minimizes the ability of their obstreperous adversaries to bother them.

CHAPTER 4

STAGE ONE: THE INFORMATION EXCHANGE

Y ou are now entering Stage One of the negotiation process: The Information Exchange. This is where you and your counterparts learn about what you have to exchange with one another. You'll notice the shift as soon as questions about each party's needs and goals replace the small talk of preliminary discussions.

Even though the primary activity of this stage is to exchange information about what you want and why you want those items, Intelligent Negotiators recognize this as a prime opportunity to create new value, to expand the pie. Try not only to discover what your counterparts want to have, but also seek ways in which you might expand your areas of mutual interest. In this way you can generate joint gains. When you create new value, by expanding the overall economic pie to be divided up, all parties are better off; you and your counterparts can simultaneously enhance your respective interests.

The Information Exchange occurs in two steps, through which you discover:

1. What are the subjects to be explored and divided?

2. What are your counterpart's needs and interests underlying those topics?

Once you know the answers to these questions, you can then determine the issues that can be addressed within the scope of your negotiations. Figure out the answer to number 1 by evaluating your situation, then evaluate the next step.

WHAT DOES YOUR COUNTERPART WANT?

The Intelligent Negotiator garners accurate information about what her opponent wants through a series of exchanges that consist of asking questions, listening for verbal leaks, and looking for nonverbal signals. Having critical information at the outset of negotiations lessens the chance that we will make erroneous assumptions about our opponents. Assumptions often turn out to be incorrect and could hinder resolution of conflict.

Ask Questions

Your general focus in the information exchange should be on the interests and desires of the *other party*. So ask questions. Spend as much time as possible asking and listening, and less time explaining your own position. Ask questions rather than speaking in declarative sentences, which do nothing but give your counterparts information. The challenge you face is to obtain as much relevant information about your counterpart's situation as possible, without disclosing too much of the confidential information pertaining to your own circumstances.

What resources and non-settlement options are available to the other side? This is what you need to know, therefore design your questions to elicit this information. If you can get away with it, casually ask what the other side plans to do if it is unable to reach a mutually acceptable agreement with you. If you succeed and your counterpart discloses his or her true BATNA (see chapter 2), you'll be able to accurately estimate how much you will ultimately have to offer to get the counterpart to accept your terms over his or her non-settlement alternatives.

There is an art to asking information-seeking questions. For instance, many negotiators make the mistake of asking narrow, focused questions that can be answered with brief "yes" or "no" responses. When this happens, the questioners tend to confirm what they already suspect. The Intelligent Negotiator gets his or her counterparts to speak, because the more they talk, the more they disclose. You can do this by asking broad, open-ended information-seeking questions that cannot be answered with brief responses. Coming up with questions such as "What do you want/need to get?" "Why are you trying to obtain those terms?" takes some planning. If you suspect there is more to the story than what your counterpart is telling you about a specific topic, try to formulate expansive inquiries covering that area. Your counterpart has no way of knowing exactly what you already know, and—let's face it—we all make the mistake of assuming that others know more than they actually know. As a result of your careful questioning, your counterpart might divulge new pieces of information, often providing leads to other areas of interest. Ask her to explain *why* she wants particular items. What interests is she seeking to satisfy? What alternatives might satisfy her underlying needs?

Once you think that you have enough general information, narrow your inquiries. Be certain that you have properly interpreted your counterpart's responses. Remember to be an *active* listener. Maintain warm and supportive eye contact with your counterpart. Nod your head while she is speaking. You may also paraphrase what she has just said to confirm what you have heard and to signal your openness to what is being disclosed. This will often lead to further disclosures. It is imperative that you listen and observe carefully. When you are either looking at your own notes or jotting down comments, you miss much of what your opponent is saying—both verbally and nonverbally. You should focus intently on the other side—listening carefully to the exact words she is using and looking for nonverbal signals that may support or contradict what she is saying orally. For example, she may nod her head affirmatively while verbally indicating that she can't agree to a particular proposal. The head nod suggests that she *can* accept that term if you are patient.

Listen for Verbal Leaks

Verbal leaks are things we say inadvertently. They are well worth listening for, as they provide extra information you can use in negotiations. Most of us feel uncomfortable when being overtly deceptive or misrepresenting actual circumstances, and we often try to avoid this moral dilemma by making statements that truthfully convey one message while inadvertently indicating something quite different. For example, in response to the question "How much do you need to sell this?" the seller might say "I *would like* to get $x" or "I'm *not inclined* to go below $x." This is very different from answering the question directly. The buyer didn't ask what the other side "wants," "would like," or is "inclined" to accept. She asked what the other side *has to have.*

When someone answers what he or she "would like" to have, "wants" to get, or is "inclined" to accept, this clues you in on the fact that your counterpart will accept less than he or she is presently demanding. Intelligent Negotiators discern these verbal leaks and appreciate their real meanings. Now you know your opponent will agree to less generous terms. When I reach my true bottom line, I never say this: "That's about as far as I can go." What I say is unequivocal and thus more credible: "That's all I have and all you will get." Whenever you hear opponents use modifiers such as "I can't go lower *at this time,*" "*I don't believe* I can go any lower," or "That's *about as* far as I can go," you can safely assume that they have more room for movement than they seem to be suggesting.

I was in the faculty lounge several years ago listening to a bargaining encounter involving two of my senior colleagues. One was trying to persuade the other to take on an onerous administrative task. The other colleague did all he could to avoid being saddled with the new responsibility, then finally said: "I'm *not inclined* to do that." I smiled, for I knew that meant he would take on the task. After more back and forth, he did indeed agree to assume responsibility for the task in question.

Speakers may also let slip their true priorities through verbal leaks. For example, if John says: "I *must have* Item 1, I *really want* Item 2, and I *would like to have* Item 3," his phrasing suggests this: Item 1 is essential; his side *must have* it. Item 2 is important, but not a deal-breaker; he really wants it, but doesn't have to have it. Item 3 is desirable, but is something he is prepared to concede for something else. Careful listeners pick up on these semantic distinctions and appreciate the priorities being disclosed. Thus if a car dealer were to say that he or she "*could not* go below $x" with respect to the basic vehicle price but "*would like* to get $y" for certain options, and "would *not be inclined* to go above $z" in terms of your trade-in, you should recognize the need to negotiate primarily in terms of the options and the trade-in value. The verbal leaks clearly indicate willingness to be flexible with respect to those two items, even though the dealer wants to obtain the base price for the unenhanced vehicle. Since you don't care whether the dealer charges you less for options or the base model, or offers you more for your trade-in, focus on the items the dealer is most likely to modify.

Here's another example: Perhaps you are leasing several floors in a large building for your company. You ask the leasing agent whether you could obtain a rent reduction based on the substantial space you are leasing, and the agent indicates an unwillingness to decrease the rent since she has promised other tenants that everyone will pay the same rent. Should you give up on your efforts? No! An Intelligent Negotiator expands the pie. First, determine where the agent's flexibility exists. Would she be willing to include cleaning services in your company's rent? Yes. Would she include utilities? Yes. By asking questions and listening carefully to the agent's stated needs, you have adroitly reduced the *cost* your firm will have to pay for the space being leased, even though you are being charged the same rent as the other building occupants.

Look for Nonverbal Signals

Be aware of nonverbal signals, for during a negotiation they are as important as verbal ones. In fact, most people find it more difficult to distort their nonverbal messages than their verbal statements. Think back to past bargaining situations, and remember times you have had the *feeling* that your opponents were interested in what you were saying or were about to change their positions. Or recall situations in which you sensed the other participants were not entirely truthful when they said they were making their "final offers." Such feelings are usually based on your subconscious reading of nonverbal signals that were either consistent or inconsistent with what the speakers were saying verbally.

True "final offers" are unlikely to be communicated by people who are sitting back in their chair, arms folded across their chest. When final offers are the real thing, the offerors are likely to be leaning slightly forward in their chair with arms extended and palms facing outward to demonstrate the openness and sincerity of their position. Verbal statements regarding final offers are only semi-believable. The verbal statements become believable when your counterparts' nonverbal signals match their concessionary words.

Do not make the mistake of failing to observe non-verbal signals. Most negotiators miss a great deal. They are either so busy focusing on other factors that they don't see nonverbal signs, or they naively think that looking for these subtle messages is unnecessary because no competent negotiator would divulge important information in such a careless manner. Anyone who harbors this opinion should read one or two of the popular books on nonverbal communication, such as *Reading People* by Jo-Ellan Dimitrius and Mark Mazzarella[1] and *Bodytalk* by Desmond Morris.[2] Once you have done some reading on nonverbal communication, watch the people around you in your office, at public events, on television, and on the street. Focus on the faces and body movements, and you will begin to see a whole new world. These cues will help you determine whether the people you are observing are happy, sad, angry, fearful, or hopeful. You will be able to discern whether your targets are patient or anxious. By training yourself to look for such signals during bargaining encounters, you will be able to ascertain important information you would otherwise miss. You must remember, however, that no single nonverbal signal is conclusive. You must look for changes in behavior and patterns of behavior that cumulatively support a particular interpretation.

Become Familiar with Classic Nonverbal Signals

What are some classic nonverbal signals worth noticing? Look at your counterpart's face. An inexperienced negotiator may actually smile when an opponent makes a generous offer or approaches the negotiator's settlement range. When this happens, you might also see a bow of the head in an attempt to conceal the smile. Most negotiators, however, are not so obvious. One person might show subtle signs of relief around the corners of the mouth when he or she begins to believe that a settlement will be achieved. Another might show tightness around the mouth, signaling tension that he or she believes present discussions are not moving satisfactorily. When someone scratches a head or brushes a cheek, this gesture may indicate puzzlement. If you receive such a response to an important message, reiterate your point in a clearer fashion.

People who are frustrated often interlock their fingers and wring their hands in a way that is painful to watch. They may grip the tabletop or the armrests on their chairs tightly. They might also bite their lip or run their fingers through their hair. Impatient people are likely to drum their fingers on the table or look frequently at their watches. As bargainers become interested in what is being said, they may move slightly forward in the chair—even so far forward that they actually place their elbows on the table in front of them.

How your counterparts respond nonverbally to new offers can be especially telling. If opponents are wholly dissatisfied with new positions, they usually respond with quick rejections and negative facial expressions. On the other hand, counterparts who are actually interested in new offers are likely to lean forward and stroke their chins, play with their glasses, or look at their notes. Even when they plan to reject the new offers, they may want to do so in an affirmative manner to keep the process going. Formulating a new, more positive rejection statement may take them ten to fifteen seconds, thus they stroke their chins, play with their glasses, and/or look at their notes to cover up the pregnant pause. When you make new offers, you should be aware of the time opponents need to respond to your position changes. When opponents begin to take longer to reply, you should suspect that they are more interested than their subsequent verbal messages may indicate.

Signs of confidence are clear indications that your counterpart believes things are progressing well. For example, he or she may engage in "steepling"—hands pressed together with fingers uplifted or together with fingers loosely interlocked and with elbows out to each side in an expansive manner. Experts pontificating on television talk shows frequently exhibit this behavior. Some individuals exhibit confidence by leaning back in their chairs with their hands behind their heads. This signal is far more likely to emanate from men than from women. When men exhibit this behavior while interacting with women, it is not only a sign of confidence but also an indication of perceived domination. Women who negotiate with male opponents exhibiting this posture should recognize this, and not be too generous.

Individuals who are eager about bargaining discussions may actually rub their hands together in an anticipatory manner. On the other hand, people who feel they are being verbally assaulted by aggressive opponents may hold their hands in front of themselves with their palms facing outward. They are symbolically—but ineffectively—trying to block the verbal onslaught coming from their adversaries.

When individuals wish to look sincere, such as when making "final offers," they may consciously or subconsciously place the palm of one hand over their heart. They may also hold out their hands with their palms facing outward to demonstrate symbolically that they have nothing to hide. When individuals attempt to fake these signals in an effort to fool naive opponents, they usually appear wooden and unnatural. If you ever have the sense that such signs are invalid, trust your intuition; it is probably based on the fact the nonverbal signs do not seem credible.

Individuals who sit with their arms folded across their chest and with their legs crossed indicate a lack of receptivity to what they hear. When the arms are folded high on the chest and one leg is crossed with the ankle on the knee of the other, this is a very competitive or combative posture, suggesting that the person is ready to do battle. Standing or sitting with hands on the hips is another combative posture. On the other hand, arms crossed low across the chest and one leg draped over the other suggests a more defensive posture. Both poses, however, represent an unreceptive attitude. These closed positions basically say, "Prove it." When you initially encounter such postures, take the time to greet those displaying them warmly with a nice handshake, since this will force them to unfold their arms. You might additionally hand them written materials that will similarly compel them to assume a more open posture.

Individuals who find it difficult to believe what you are saying may casually rub one eye with one or two fingers. When you encounter such a nonverbal response to a truthful statement, restate what you just said. You may also support the questioned statement with corroborative factual information.

Eye contact can be especially informative. Some individuals stare intently at negotiating counterparts when bargaining begins, suggesting that they are highly competitive people who are ready to do battle. On rare occasions, the staring may be so intense that it is intimidating or even threatening. Other people make warm eye contact that says they optimistically anticipate mutually beneficial discussions. People who make good eye contact when speaking tend to look far more truthful than individuals who rarely look into the eyes of others.

Identify Outright Lies and Other Deceptions

In his classic book *Telling Lies*,[3] Paul Ekman asserts that when people lie they experience stress, and that stress can be detected from their nonverbal signs. Signs of such stress include arms and legs moving more rapidly than usual, more frequent eye blinking, a higher pitched voice, frequent clearing of the throat, and increased speech errors (stuttering, repeating phrases, or trailing off without completing the entire thought being expressed).

Most of us have been raised to believe that lying is reprehensible. As a result, when we begin to distort the truth, we sometimes involuntarily place a hand over our mouth as if we are subconsciously trying to hold in the lie we know is morally wrongful. Many of us shake our heads slowly when dishonestly saying yes and meaning no, or nod our head slowly when saying no and meaning yes.

What conduct might liars use to enhance the believability of their planned misrepresentations? Beware when you hear such signal phrases as "to be truthful" or "to be candid." Such phrases are designed to induce you to listen more intently to the lie they are about to utter. Statements following such expressions are likely to be anything but truthful or candid! Persons trying to look more credible may obviously decrease their gross body movement to look less fidgety or deliberately look into the eyes of people with whom they have not made good eye contact. They may speak more slowly to be certain their opponents hear them.

When you have the sense your opponents are not being candid, ask yourself whether you have observed any of these signs. Review the other objective information you have to determine whether that contradicts what you have just been told. When negotiating, learn to trust your feelings. You will usually do better when you are paying attention to nonverbal messages.

MORE TECHNIQUES FOR INFORMATION RETRIEVAL

Your most important task during the information exchange is to gather information. The best way to elicit information is simple: *Ask a lot of questions.* When people talk in response to your questions, they divulge both direct and indirect pieces of information. *Direct* information is what is expressly stated, such as "My budget for this item is $x." *Indirect* information is implicit from what is said as well as what is not said. Indirect information also includes factual matters hinted about by negotiators and information that may be surmised because of the other side's unwillingness to address certain matters. For instance, if you ask several specific questions pertaining to particular areas and your adversaries keep changing the subject in an obvious effort to avoid answering your inquiries, you may reasonably suspect that the true answers, if given, would favor your side.

Once you think you have gleaned enough general information from your counterparts to move ahead, use more specific questions to confirm your current understandings.

Restate the responses you think you have received from them, so they can confirm, modify, or reject your interpretations of their prior statements. In some instances, counterparts may use blocking techniques to avoid direct responses to your specific questions—ignoring them, misinterpreting them, or otherwise trying to change the subject. Don't allow them to use evasive behavior to deny you the information you deserve. Whenever adversaries refuse to fully answer your questions, restate and ask again.

Keep in mind that if you plan to listen and watch your counterparts as carefully as possible during the information exchange, try to take as few notes as possible. When you look at your notes or write down comments in your notes, you miss much of what is being "said" verbally and nonverbally. It is difficult to read and listen at the same time. It is virtually impossible to write and listen simultaneously. Even when we think we are concentrating on what other people are saying, we do not understand all of their signals. We are thinking about what was said a minute earlier and what we should say next, and therefore miss what is being said at that very moment.

The next stage of your negotiations will be value claiming. Many negotiators make the mistake of rushing the information exchange to get into Stage Two (which I'll cover in chapter 5). Although you may be tempted to do so, don't. You need a thorough information exchange to truly evaluate and structure an intelligent deal. If you discuss the concessions you are willing to make before having all the basic information to formulate a beneficial accord, you will lose out. Make sure you take the time to have a comprehensive information exchange. If you think opponents possess additional information that may be helpful, ask more questions. When you do not receive direct answers, ask the questions again. There is no limit on questions. If you suspect you haven't been given all the information, ask more questions.

Here is a good example of what can happen when you don't ask enough questions. In my classes I present the following negotiation exercise, based on a real case: The plaintiff sustains several broken bones in an automobile accident, which appear to have healed. When the defense attorney has a physician examine the plaintiff to enable him to testify as an expert witness for the defense, the doctor discovers a life-threatening aneurism on the plaintiff's aorta.

I have had thousands of practicing lawyers work on this exercise, and no more than 5 percent of plaintiff attorneys bother to ask the defense counsel what their doctor discovered—even though they know that the physician has examined their client and they are entitled to that information. On those rare occasions when plaintiff lawyers ask the right question, they are oblivious to the fact that their opponents ignore the question or focus on other areas and fail to provide the requested information. In the real case, the plaintiff's lawyer failed to ask the critical question, and the case was settled without the plaintiff or his attorney being aware of the plaintiff's life-threatening condition.

WHO MAKES THE FIRST OFFER?

Are you wondering whether to disclose your position first or try to get your opponents to do so? Some bargainers (particularly Cooperators) like to state their own positions at the outset because they think that beginning with reasonable positions will encourage similar behavior by opponents. While this can be quite effective when negotiating with friends and business partners, it is risky with respect to counterparts you do not really know. When you take that first step, you depend on counterparts to reciprocate with realistic opening offers of their own. An Adversary or an Innovator will probably not respond in kind. Adversarial counterparts are more likely to exploit your forthrightness by stating a less generous position, placing you on the defensive. For instance, if you begin close to the settlement range and they respond with an offer quite a ways outside that range, you will find it psychologically draining to force them to make consistently larger concessions than you are making. As a result, manipulative adversaries can use your willingness to go first to their own advantage and obtain more generous terms from you than you might otherwise have provided.

If you are uncertain what the exact scope of the settlement range is, get your counterpart to state her position first. You may discover that you have been too generous toward her in your preliminary assessment of the operative circumstances, or that she has been too generous toward you. Whoever goes first will disclose this miscalculation, allowing the other party to take advantage of the situation. Proficient negotiators put themselves in this position whenever possible.

For example, when my wife and I first moved to Washington, D.C., we purchased a townhouse and went shopping to find a used secretary for our dining room. We visited a furniture dealer in Northern Virginia and found a lovely piece on sale for $1,150. I thought of making a $1,000 offer to see whether the dealer would be willing to compromise on the asking price, but decided instead to ask him what he would accept if we were prepared to make a purchase on the spot. My wife and I were shocked when he responded with a figure of $800! I doubt he would have responded with an $800 counteroffer had I initially proposed $1,000. Although I then responded to his $800 offer with a counter of $750, he made it clear that he would not be willing to go below $800, the amount we finally paid. By getting the dealer to go first, we saved a minimum of $200 and perhaps as much as $300 to $350, since we were perfectly willing to pay the full $1,150 asking price.

When you induce your counterpart to make the first offer, you gain another advantage: You can then engage in *bracketing*. Use bracketing to make counteroffers that place your goal near the mid-point between the parties' initial offers. Bracketing narrows the range of your discussions, manipulating the mid-range to your advantage. For example, if you hope to pay $500 for something and the seller begins with an asking price of $575, you offer $425 to keep your $500 target at the center of your respective opening offers. This works as often as it does because most bargainers feel a psychological obligation to move from the first offers toward the center. Even if your counterparts do not move all the way to the mid-point, they may move further in your direction than they would have if you had either gone first or had begun with a counteroffer that did not place your target price in the middle.

If you can induce your opponents to make the first offer, you are also more likely to induce them to make the first concession. Studies indicate that individuals who make the first concession during bargaining encounters do less well than their opponents.[4] These persons tend to be more anxious negotiators who are afraid they will not achieve agreements if they do not move quickly. They thus make more and larger concessions than their more

patient adversaries. But the logistics of discussion favor
this as well: After their initial offer and your counteroffer,
it is natural for you to look back to them for the first concession; it is their turn to disclose the next position. This
approach increases the probability that they will make a
greater number of concessions than you make.

When opponents begin with offers that are more generous than you anticipated, you must act quickly to take
advantage of the situation. Modify your planned opening
offer in your favor to skew the discussions in your direction. You are in the position to take advantage of the fact
they think you deserve a better deal than you believe you
should get. Don't hesitate to defer to the superior judgment of opponents who conclude that you are entitled to
more than you had hoped to achieve!

I have a friend who represents plaintiffs in medical
malpractice cases. He had a client with a claim he thought
was worth $75,000. When he began the serious discussions
with the insurance company representative, it became
clear that his opponent thought the claim was worth more
than he did. He immediately raised both his aspiration
level and his planned opening demand to take advantage
of this unexpected development. He finally settled his
"$75,000 case" for $250,000. When he was done, his only
concern was whether he could have obtained more. The insurance company representative must have known something that he did not. For example, the representative may
have known that the treating physician was drug- or alco-
hol-impaired when he treated the claimant. My friend had
no information of this kind, but he was certainly willing to
accept his opponent's unanticipated generosity.

If you are sitting across the table from an adversarial negotiator, chances are that your counterpart will
begin with a wholly unrealistic offer favoring him or her-

self. What should you do when this happens? Don't make the mistake of responding to unreasonable opening offers in a casual manner. That behavior may allow your counterpart to think his or her positions are not outrageous. When negotiators begin with absurd positions, they almost always know that their offers are outlandish, and they expect you to say something negative about their position. If you fail to do so in a forceful way, they begin to think their unrealistic offers are acceptable—and they raise their expectation level. If your counterpart opens this way, politely but forcefully indicate your displeasure with his or her opening position. Tell this person directly that the offer is untenable. This type of negotiator expects you to do so and actually feels comfortable when you do. They are merely information gathering in an extremely aggressive manner.

In some instances, you will be able to persuade counterparts who have made opening offers to "bid against themselves" by making additional offers. Try this by asking: "Is that the best you can do?" or alternatively: "You'll have to do better than that, because . . ." If you provide them with a reason to make you another offer (for example, you have received a better offer from a competing party), they may give you a more generous position statement. If you are lucky, a careless counterpart may make several concessions before you even state your own opening position. Another way to generate the same effect is to employ the strategic use of silence. Following opening offers or subsequent concessions, look dejected and remain silent, and you will be amazed how often counterparts fill the voids with additional position changes.

Is there an easy way to induce counterparts to make the first offer? Unfortunately, there is not. In some circumstances, however, we expect one side to go first as a matter of common practice. For example, people who put their house on the market are expected to provide a listing, or asking price. Retailers are supposed to list or state the price of the commodities they are selling. Employers offering applicants new positions are usually expected to either list in the job announcement, or state in the job offer the salary involved. Other than these types of situations, the marketplace does not suggest who should go first. When the time comes, remember the advantages to be gained when you induce your counterpart to make the first offer.

PUTTING YOUR PRIORITIES IN PLACE

The Intelligent Negotiator wishes to maximize the joint return of both parties. To do this, you must know which items are most and least valued by your counterparts. Like your goal priorities (the ones you set in chapter 2), your counterparts' priorities are critical. Listen carefully to discover what they are.

Identify Conflicting Priorities

The various items to be exchanged can be classified as "essential," "important," and "desirable." Which terms do they feel they *must* have, they strongly *wish* to have, and would merely *like* to have? Once you and your counterparts begin to disclose your respective values, you can evaluate the degree to which your own objectives conflict with the goals of the other side. In some instances, both of you may actually desire the identical distribution of the

Table 1   **JOINT NEEDS COMPARISON**

	Shared Needs	Independent Needs		Conflicting Needs	
		Side A	Side B	Side A	Side B
Essential Needs					
Important Needs					
Desirable Needs					

items in question, allowing you to enhance your respective interests simultaneously. Through an appropriate resolution of these *"shared needs,"* you can maximize the joint return.

In their book *Interviewing, Counseling, and Negotiating,*[5] Professors Robert Bastrass and Joseph Harbaugh created a table that graphically highlights the different levels of party needs (see table 1).

You may discover that one side desires items that are of no particular interest to the other side. The participant who values the items should be given these terms. Why would the other side be so generous? Being accommodating with respect to items the other side values and you do not can increase the likelihood that you will get other terms that you value. By resolving these *independent needs* appropriately, each side enhances the likelihood that it will obtain the terms it prefers.

Proficient negotiators should work to ascertain the areas of *shared* and *independent needs* to ensure the proper distribution of these non-conflicted items. When negotiators attempt to resolve disputes over their *conflicted needs*, they must try to remember the degree to which they actually want these items. If one side considers a disputed matter "essential" while the other views it as "important" or "desirable," the term should be given to the side that values it more in exchange for something the other side considers more significant. For example, if a prospective employee considers three weeks of vacation critical but the hiring company does not, while the company is absolutely unwilling to provide employees with company cars, the employee would be better off trading her claim to a company vehicle for an extra week of vacation, enabling both parties to obtain the items they value more.

When negotiating parties encounter direct conflicts involving items that both sides value equally, they must look for appropriate compromises. If there are several issues of this kind, the parties may agree to divide them up. Or one may concede one "essential" term for two or three "important" items. For example, a car dealer may agree to include a better audio system for a higher price. The buyer values the system at the $450 retail price, while the dealer values it at the $300 dealer cost. If one participant tries to claim all the conflicted items, an unproductive impasse is likely to result. It thus behooves both parties to look for ways in which the conflicted issues can be resolved amicably rather than place one side in a position that requires them to do all the yielding. An effort should always be made to generate compromises that provide each side with the sense that it got some of what it really wanted in exchange for concessions on other desired items.

Competitive/adversarial negotiators, particularly those with a win-lose mentality, may be hesitant to accept a cooperative approach. They may think that their aggressive tactics will enable them to claim more "essential" and "important" items for themselves. While they may occasionally achieve such skewed results from less proficient or naive opponents, they can rarely hope to do so against skilled adversaries. Furthermore, when ongoing relationships are involved, those who regularly claim the lion's share of items for themselves may find their personal and professional relationships deteriorating. Before they know it, they may find themselves divorced from their spouses or business partners.

Competitive negotiators should appreciate the benefits that can be derived from win-win bargaining techniques. To the extent that you can satisfy opponent interests at minimal or no cost to yourself, you can greatly increase the likelihood of mutually beneficial results. You can also enhance your ability to claim more of the conflicted items for yourself. So long as you are able to obtain what you really value, you should not be disappointed by the fact that your opponent's interests have also been satisfied. Instead of asking whether you did better than your opponent, ask whether you are pleased with what you got. The fact that your adversary did worse is of little consolation if you also failed to attain beneficial results.

MULTIPLE-ITEM NEGOTIATIONS

Multiple-item negotiations—such as those involving long-term projects, employment contracts, or even divorce proceedings—are complex. Here are a few factors you should keep in mind to be as effective a negotiator as possible. Watch how your counterparts begin this stage of the discussion. Since negotiating over ten or twenty items simultaneously is impossible, multiple-item negotiators break their discussion into manageable segments of three or four topics per segment. Most negotiators begin the talks with a group of either their most or their least important terms, rarely mixing important and unimportant topics. Anxious negotiators usually begin with their most valued terms, hoping to resolve them quickly. This is a risky approach. Both sides may value many of the same items, and when one party begins with the most hotly disputed topics, participants may reach a quick impasse and conclude that the gulf between them is too great to achieve a mutual accord.

Intelligent Negotiators generally prefer to begin the bargaining process with a discussion of the *less significant* topics for these reasons:

1. They want to generate quick agreement on these less controversial items. If things progress well, they should be able to reach tentative agreements on many, if not most, of these terms before they get to the more conflicted items.

2. They want to create a psychological commitment to the bargaining process. By initially focusing on the areas of agreement, rather than the areas of disagreement, these parties are able to agree—tentatively—on many terms, creating a psychological commitment to the bargaining process. As they move toward the more controversial topics, they remember how many terms have already been resolved, and the remaining items no longer seem insurmountable.

Look closely at the groups of items with which your counterparts initiate the serious talks. If they open the discussions with a group of four items, three of which are insignificant to you, but one of which you value, your opponents probably consider all four to be relatively unimportant. If you can exchange the term you value for one or two of the other items during the preliminary exchange, you will obtain a real gain at minimal cost to yourself.

On the other hand, if opponents begin with four items, three of which you value and one of which you do not, they probably value all four terms. Try to trade the item you do not value for one of the three you consider important. Don't feel guilty about the fact that you may be obtaining a valuable term for something you do not personally value. When determining the importance of bargaining chips, remember this: The value of items being exchanged is in the eye of the beholder. If I have something you want, you will pay a reasonable price to get it. If you don't value what I possess, you will give me nothing important for it even if others indicate that they think the item is valuable.

Overstating and Understating Value

Do not forget that fellow negotiators—even friends and business associates in some cases—may employ deceptive bargaining tactics to obtain an advantage. They may overstate or understate the value of certain items for strategic reasons. As you might do yourself (as discussed above), when your bargaining counterparts think you value something they don't care about, they may indicate an interest in that term. Conversely, if they believe you don't want something, they may suggest a similar lack of interest in that topic, even though they actually value it. This behavior, *puffing* and *embellishment,* is an inherent part of most negotiations. As long as the *puffing* and *embellishment* do not go entirely beyond the bounds of propriety, few would consider such tactics reprehensible.

When you prepare for negotiations, it is important to ascertain the reputations of your counterparts with respect to honesty. Are they individuals who can be trusted when they talk about what you have the right to know? Do they shade the truth in inappropriate ways? While some disingenuousness is to be expected, outright dishonesty is not. If you have reason to mistrust particular negotiators, be wary of what they tell you. Try to obtain independent verification of important representations, and only believe what you are able to confirm. If you believe the lies of people you know are dishonest, the fault is your own.

Another way to gauge truthfulness is to listen carefully for verbal leaks that may provide important clues to the speaker's real values. Also look for nonverbal signs that may confirm or contradict what is being said verbally. For instance, when the verbal and nonverbal signals are congruent, you can usually believe those consistent signals. When, however, the verbal and nonverbal signals conflict, you can generally rely on the nonverbal messages since actions and facial expressions are more difficult to fake than words. Trust your feelings; they often reflect subconscious reading of nonverbal clues. When discrepancies do arise, proceed to ask more questions, and apply common sense. Does it make sense to think your opponent doesn't value something you believe is important or prefers something you think is worthless?

Determining Your Important Information

When you prepare for your bargaining encounter, you must determine what information you plan to disclose and how you can most effectively disclose it. Do not forget to also determine what information you would prefer to withhold, and how you can best protect it. Consider these issues *before* you interact with opponents, to avoid mistakes caused by incomplete planning.

Controlling Disclosure of Your Own Information

During the information exchange, both parties have to disclose some information or the negotiation process is not going to develop effectively. But you are naïve if you divulge your important information up front, even if your intention is to demonstrate your straightforward bargaining style. You might find manipulative disclosure strategies distasteful, and therefore try to avoid them; however, you will also stand a good chance of being disappointed in the results you achieve. Volunteering your own important information too quickly without obtaining similar candor from your counterparts will create an information imbalance favoring your counterparts, who now hold more important information about you than you have about them.

Such straightforward disclosure may create an additional problem. It might not even occur to your counterparts that a proficient bargainer would be so quick to unilaterally disclose such important information. This produces *reactive devaluation,* in which your counterparts jump to the conclusion that you are trying to confuse them by withholding other more critical information. As they look for the information that has not been addressed, they may miss what was actually said and devalue what they heard.

Intelligent Negotiators who want counterparts to hear and respect their important information should play the game. Don't volunteer critical information. Instead, let your information out slowly in response to your counterpart's questions. When people ask questions, two things happen:

1. The questioner listens more intently to what you have to say because your answers pertain to their questions. They thus hear more of what you are saying.

2. They attribute your disclosures to their questioning ability and accord what they hear greater respect. If you want your counterparts to hear and respect more of your valuable information, make them work for it. Let it out slowly in response to their inquiries.

A friend recently provided me with a great example of *reactive devaluation*. While representing his company in collective bargaining talks with the union representing firm employees, he and the union agent had proposed different language for a new seniority system that would determine employee job security and affect promotional opportunities. He did not like the union proposals, and they did not like his suggested terms. In an effort to break the deadlock, he reiterated his primary concerns and told the union agent he would accept any provision they formulated in good faith. Several days later, the union negotiator gave him their new proposal. The company negotiator examined it and indicated the reservations he still had. He then indicated that he would accept their good faith effort to resolve the matter. At this point, the union agent rose, tore up his own proposal, and said: "If it's acceptable to you, it must not be good for us." He stormed out of the office. Even though he had drafted the provision in question, the union representative figured that if the proposal was all right for the company, it should be rejected by the union!

Using Blocking Techniques to Avoid Answering Sensitive Questions

What can you do when people across the table ask questions about topics and areas you would prefer not to discuss? You can use *blocking* techniques to avoid answering without making it obvious that you are not responding. For example, you can simply ignore a question you don't like and continue the discussion where it was before. If you do this casually, your counterparts may become re-engaged in the talks you have continued and forget that you never responded to their inquiry. When you are given a compound question containing several parts, you can focus on the portion of the question you like and ignore the rest. As counterparts become involved with your limited answer, they may fail to return to the unanswered portions of their initial question.

To be effective, strive to maintain a calm and pleasant demeanor when using blocking techniques. You may be able to over- or under-answer questions you don't like. If someone targets a specific issue, you can provide a general response. For example, when discussing the possible starting salary for a new position, if you are asked the exact salary you would need to get to make the job attractive, you could respond that you would expect to be paid what other workers at this firm or at comparable firms are paid for such work. At the other end of the spectrum, you might be asked your general employment goals over the next ten years and respond with a desire to learn the tasks associated with the immediate position before you contemplate other opportunities.

You can occasionally misinterpret a question you don't like and answer the inquiry you have reformulated. For example, a prospective employer may ask you about your current salary, which you think does not reflect your true value. You could suggest that the questioner really wants to know what salary you must receive for the position you are considering and respond to the rephrased inquiry. If you do this adroitly, the asker may forget to seek further information about your present salary. You could alternatively respond to such a question with a question of your own. When asked about your current salary, you could ask the questioner about the compensation range for the position you are discussing. If you can induce that person to talk about this issue, she may fail to realize that you never responded to her initial inquiry.

In rare cases, potential employers may ask about information you consider personal or confidential, such as questions about your family care arrangements, or questions they may have no legal right to ask, such as your age. Don't be afraid to let them know that you consider this an inappropriate question that you will not answer. If you state your position politely, but forcefully, the questioner will probably yield to your desire for privacy and not take offense by your unwillingness to reply.

If you plan your use of blocking techniques in advance and prepare to vary them, you will be amazed how often you can avoid responding to questions you believe will undermine your situation. You might ignore one question, partially answer a later inquiry, and misinterpret a subsequent probe. If you learn to use blocking devices naturally, opponents will rarely recognize what you are doing. Watch good politicians on Sunday morning talk shows. At the conclusion of their appearances, ask yourself what specific information they have provided. They are masters at avoiding difficult questions without being obvious that they are not being forthright. This is a skill that all proficient negotiators should know how to use.

Remember the psychological impact of gain-loss framing that was discussed in chapter 2 as you begin to discuss the particular items to be exchanged. This can be quite helpful as a persuasive technique to bolster your arguments. Frame your answers in terms of *sure gains,* rather than *probable losses.* When people are forced to choose between the two, they normally select the certain benefits.

For instance a recent encounter between my wife, Katey, and a street vendor selling flowers graphically demonstrates this. She was contemplating the purchase of a lovely bouquet, but considered the $15 asking price excessive. She attempted to talk the vendor into a lower price, but he refused to budge. She finally took a $10 bill out of her pocket, held it in front of herself, and said that was all she had. The seller focused on the $10 bill and decided that a certain gain was preferable to the mere possibility of a greater gain from a future buyer. He thus took her $10 bill and handed her the bouquet!

Finding Common Ground

Too many negotiators are purely adversarial, as we discussed in chapter 1. They lock themselves into set positions and defend those positions with strident arguments. They try to intimidate their opponents into complete capitulation. They ignore counterparts' statements that conflict with their preconceived ideas and fail to acknowledge alternative proposals that could prove mutually beneficial.

When a fairly broad settlement range exists between two or more parties' respective bottom lines, the parties should be able to achieve mutual accords. But adversarial behavior, or bargaining in a closed and competitive manner, lessens the likelihood that negotiators will be able to do so. If you and your counterparts have developed a more open and cooperative information exchange, such as the Cooperator or Innovator styles of negotiating, you may discover efficient alternatives that would work to the benefit of both sides.

In bargaining situations in which the settlement range is fairly limited, you are very likely to encounter difficulty when you seek a zone of agreement. Try not to focus excessively on your areas of conflict. Instead, look for common ground—so that you can expand the pie to be divided between you and your bargaining counterpart and enhance the probability of agreement.

You can accomplish this by formulating open inquiries intended to encourage expanded participation. It is crucial that you and your fellow negotiants trust each other enough so you will be able to explore your respective interests and goals at the table. In this situation, objective questions can be quite helpful in reviewing each side's understanding of the relevant factual and economic circumstances. If you and your counterpart can agree upon these basic factors in a noncompetitive manner, you are on your way to achieving mutually beneficial results.

Each side needs to appreciate the hidden pressures influencing the other. Are financial or emotional factors constraining your counterpart's flexibility? Are these factors more imagined than real? If so, a careful exploration of each negotiator's concerns may be sufficient to assuage fears. If the concerns are valid, they have to be addressed. Don't be afraid to tell your counterpart what is really bothering you because you have little hope of ending a stalemate if you do not.

Looking for Ways to Expand the Pie

Don't assume that what you want is what your opponents want. While both parties may value some of the same items (money, for example), they may not value these terms equally. In addition, there are usually a number of items valued by one side but not by the other. If the negotiators can ascertain and exploit these preference differences, they can improve their respective positions. For example, a famous negotiating story features two siblings fighting over the single orange they possess. Both attempt to obtain the orange to satisfy their needs, but neither is willing to yield. They finally agree to what seems the only rational solution available to them. They cut the orange down the middle and each gets one half. Only later do they discover that one wanted the pulp to make juice, while the other wanted the rind to make zest! Had they explored these underlying interests earlier, both could have maximized their return by having one take all the pulp and the other all the rind. By not exploring their actual needs, each party walked away with far less than he or she could have satisfactorily gained.

I recall a labor arbitration in which the company had adopted a no-fault absentee policy without consulting the union that represented its employees. The parties got to the hearing I was conducting and could not agree on the issue to be resolved. The company lawyer said he could not understand what the union wanted, and the union attorney said the company should have talked with them before adopting the policy. The company lawyer stated that the union would have opposed any policy, but the union attorney replied that they would not have done so given the firm's high absentee rate. The company lawyer then asked *why* the union was complaining about the policy the firm had adopted. The union attorney said that if a worker were seriously ill or had major surgery, he or she would lose the job since the policy allowed no "excused" absences. The company lawyer responded that it would never apply the policy in such an inhumane way. The parties then redrafted the policy to close this unintended loophole. The company was certain the union opposed any absentee policy, but this was not the case. The union was sure the company intended to terminate workers with serious medical problems, but that was not the company's intention. Once they understood each other's underlying concerns, they had no difficulty drafting mutually acceptable language.

For example, you are meeting with investors for your fledgling company. Your common ground is that both sides want the company to grow solidly toward the IPO stage. You propose to hire more staff in order to build a solid operations base, but your investors are pushing for you to spend less money. In cases such as this, look for ways to expand the overall pie. Since most negotiators value the various items being discussed quite differently, trade-offs can usually be found that simultaneously benefit both sides. In this situation, you might explore the possibility of a more ambitious IPO than originally planned—one that includes a stronger, more solid operations division for your company (a better value for shareholders). Or perhaps as founder you will explore the possibility of taking less personal compensation in exchange for a greater number of shares once the company has gone public.

Once the participants have identified their respective underlying interests, they can begin to search for mutually beneficial settlement terms. Through brainstorming, the parties can look for new options that effectively enlarge the pie. But before you engage in brainstorming, be sure to establish some ground rules. Encourage each side to suggest possible alternatives the participants think would enhance the underlying needs of each party. Neither party should be allowed to criticize specific proposals until both sides have had the opportunity to disclose all alternatives they may be contemplating. This encourages complete openness.

Felicia puts many bargaining strategies into practice in her negotiations with Andersen. After Vice President Solomon and Felicia exchange pleasantries, he describes the present situation at Andersen. Their retail stores are doing well, and catalog sales are increasing each year. Although their dot-com business has been going on for a little more than a year, they are doing better than initially anticipated. They need a network manager who can manage their warehouse inventories and help them expand their business. Solomon acknowledges Felicia's excellent educational background, and admits that her high school teaching experience is viewed positively since she would have to interact with many people who are not techies. His directness puts Felicia at ease. She indicates how pleased she is to have an offer from such an outstanding firm. The fact they are expanding their e-business is especially attractive to her.

Solomon says that he doesn't like to haggle too much about salary levels, and says he would like to begin the discussions with an offer of $58,000. Since Felicia had expected him to begin in the $55,000 to $57,000 area, she feels optimistic. His "begin the discussion" language suggests some degree of flexibility regarding salary. She casually indicates that other firms are paying network managers in the $70,000 range—to place that figure in his mind. She then asks about fringe benefits. Solomon says they would provide complete health coverage, two weeks of vacation, and contribute 8 percent of her salary to a pension fund. He emphasizes that the network manager generally works from 8:30 a.m. until 5:15 p.m., except on rare days when real network problems are encountered. In addition, the network manager has two assistants who help keep the various systems operating.

Felicia asks if Andersen covers new employee moving expenses, training courses, or the cost of a company car. He responds that they have no specific policies pertaining to moving expenses or training programs, but notes that no workers are provided with company transportation. She asks whether Andersen ever provides "signing bonuses" to new employees and is pleased when Solomon says they "are not inclined to do so."

Solomon asks Felicia what salary she would need to accept the Andersen position. She doesn't wish to give him a definitive figure at this early stage of their interaction. She thus replies that she is looking for a salary in the mid-$60,000 range. When he does not immediately reject this stated goal, she begins to think she might obtain something approaching $65,000.

Felicia asks Solomon if Andersen has a stock option plan or performance bonuses. He says that they have a stock option program enabling employees to purchase stock at preferred prices. He also indicates that store salespeople work on a commission basis, and suggests that other personnel could receive performance-based payments.

SUMMARY POINTS

- During the Information Exchange, the parties try to determine what is available to be exchanged.

- Focus on what your counterpart really wants. The best way to elicit such information is to ask broad, open-ended information seeking questions and listen actively. Negotiators may do this by listening for "verbal leaks" that inadvertently disclose important information about speaker positions and priorities, and looking for nonverbal signals that convey important information and may suggest the presence of deceptive behavior.

- It is beneficial to get your opponent to make the first offer, to see how he or she views the relevant circumstances, and to allow you to "bracket" your goal with an opening offer that places your goal halfway between the opening positions of the parties.

- When multiple-item negotiations are involved, skilled negotiators begin the serious discussions with less important items to encourage quick agreement on these items and generate a joint psychological commitment to agreement.

- Proficient negotiators disclose their important information in response to opponent questions to enhance the value of what they are disclosing, and they use "blocking" techniques to avoid answering sensitive questions.

(continues)

SUMMARY POINTS (CONTINUED)

- Skilled negotiators seek common ground, going behind the stated positions in search of the interests underlying those positions, so they can explore alternative solutions that may be mutually beneficial.

- Good negotiators realize that most bargaining encounters do not involve fixed pies; they seek ways to expand the pie and simultaneously enhance the interests of both sides.

CHAPTER 5

STAGE TWO: THE DISTRIBUTIVE STAGE

The focus of the discussion now changes from what your counterparts wish to achieve to what you hope to get for yourself. You are entering the Distributive Stage of your encounter, where you begin to divide up the items on the table. While the Information Exchange you just completed in Stage One consists of *value creation,* when the parties determine what is available be divided up, stage two represents *value claiming,* when you and your counterparts claim the items you found during the first stage.

THE COMPETITIVE NATURE OF THE DISTRIBUTIVE STAGE

The transition between these two stages, creating and claiming value, is usually easy to spot. Each bargainer be-

gins talking about his or her own side's needs. Often negotiators' body language changes from relaxed and cordial to
less relaxed and more aggressive. Be alert. You are about
to enter the stage of the bargaining process that determines what each side ultimately receives. The distributive
stage is the most competitive part of the bargaining
process because both parties are claiming the items on the
table. And rarely are the participants trying to divide the
available items in a wholly equitable manner. Negotiators
using an adversarial negotiating style often have an advantage here. Cooperators need to adapt their style during this stage because emphasizing the win-win approach
essentially ignores the distributive nature of the bargaining encounter. The Cooperative Problem-Solving technique is effective with respect to the less controversial
items, but it works poorly with the terms that *both sides*
want. There is no way these conflicted issues can be completely shared; you must compete for these terms. If a Cooperator naively considers the process a pure win-win
endeavor and is too open with an adversarial counterpart,
he or she is likely to be cleaned out during the bargaining
process. It would be like two people playing a game of
poker in which one has to play with his cards face up during the betting while the other is allowed to hide her
cards! The best style in this highly competitive stage is a
hybrid style such as that of the Innovator who will match
his or her counterpart's level of information disclosure.

Objective standards that you can use to determine
exactly what each side "deserves" are seldom available.
Moreover, individuals tend to seek more than their fair
share. While the most equitable solution might be to divide the items equally, this ignores the fact that participants rarely possess equal bargaining power and identical
skill. Negotiators with greater strength and ability will al-

most always be able to obtain better terms than their weaker adversaries. For example, someone might be trying to sell a house during a poor economic cycle. The house cost the owner $250,000 to buy, plus he has since added $200,000 worth of improvements. The owner would feel satisfied if he received $350,000 for it, but realizes that there may be no buyers willing to pay that price. Would it be inappropriate for a prospective buyer to offer $300,000 if she considered that a reasonable price in light of the other houses currently on the market? Should she be morally obliged to offer more just because the seller would lose so much on a sale at that price?

One mode of thought suggests that negotiators should attempt to come out in the "middle." The problem with this strategy is that it assumes each side has equal merit—financial, social, moral, and otherwise. This is rarely the case. For example, if an employer has refused to hire someone because of his or her race, gender, age, or disability, should the victim of this discrimination have to accept less than full lost wages to make the final settlement "fair" to the discriminating firm?

Let Objective Criteria Guide You

An infinitely more fair, useful, and effective distributive standard is to create solutions based on principle, evaluating items and their distribution by objective standards. Objective standards could be market value, scientific standards, governmental standards, legal decisions, or community standards of fairness and reciprocity, to name a few.

Take the example of the house sale mentioned above. If the participants were to use objective standards that conversation might go like this:

BUYER: We are willing to pay $300,000 for this house.

SELLER: I appreciate your offer. However, we have added $200,000 of improvements here over the past ten years. Even if we get $350,000, we will never recoup that.

BUYER: Your improvements are solid and certainly enhance the value of this house, although you must admit that some of them were long overdue. We happen to know that comparable houses are priced at $300,000.

SELLER: I know that, too. But there is no way we can let our house go at that price.

BUYER: Hmm. This house really fits our needs. If you agree to sell it to us for $325,000, we have a deal.

SELLER: All right.

Both parties acknowledge that the relevant value of this house is determined by what the market price is, and allow other considerations to flow from that figure.

The use of objective criteria can be so effective in a highly competitive stage because it lessens our reliance on hard bargaining, and provides a rational basis for the exchange agreed upon by both parties.

Create a Concession Strategy

If you are to walk away from the table with the terms you really want, you need to plan your position changes so they are carefully formulated and strategically disclosed. This planning will be your concession strategy. The con-

cession strategy serves as a blueprint, allowing you to determine ahead of time the size and timing of your position
changes, what your rational explanations for these
changes will be, and whether you can anticipate making
several larger concessions or a series of smaller changes.

The elements of a successful concession strategy include consistent use of principled positions, a self-confi-
dent approach, prior knowledge of the size and timing of
your position changes, and your own as well as your counterpart's non-settlement alternatives.

Know the Importance of Self-Confidence

Self-assurance is a common attribute among successful
negotiators. They always appear to be in control of themselves and their bargaining encounters. How do you accomplish this display of confidence? Carefully evaluate
your non-settlement options before meeting with your opponents. Once you know your options, you will not be
afraid. Your fellow negotiators are likely to be influenced
by your inner confidence. If your counterparts begin to
think that their own non-settlement alternatives look a
lot less rosy than the options available to you, they are
likely to feel greater pressure to reach agreements. That's
when they start to make more and larger concessions.

When self-confidence wanes, as it does even with the
most self-assured among us, and you doubt your own bargaining power, you should do two things:

1. Ask yourself what weaknesses your opponents
   have that they are hiding. They are projecting
   their strengths, and you must try to estimate the
   weaknesses they are concealing.

2. Reassess your own circumstances to ask what strengths *you* are projecting. If you are doing a good job of disguising your own problem areas, your adversaries may believe you possess more power than *you* think you do! Reconsider your own non-settlement options, and try to refocus on the alternatives that are available to your opponents. Try not to attribute imaginary strength to your adversaries.

When I work with attorneys as a negotiation consultant, they do a wonderful job of explaining their own side's weaknesses. When I place myself in the shoes of their opponents and articulate the problems they have to confront, the lawyers with whom I am working are shocked. They have completely failed to consider the difficulties affecting their opponents. At this point, they begin to appreciate the bargaining power they possess.

Use Principled Positions When Making Concessions

Position changes must be carefully formulated and strategically disclosed. When properly used, a concession can signal both a cooperative attitude and sufficient firmness to indicate the need for a counteroffer should the negotiator intend to continue the negotiation process. Intelligent Negotiators begin the distributive stage with principled positions that rationally explain the basis for what they want. Plan to make principled concessions you can rationally explain to your counterparts. When you put a new position on the table, explain why you have decided to make that particular move. You may suggest that you have under- or over-valued a specific item by a certain amount—and then change your current position accordingly. You may alternatively indicate that you have failed to adequately consider a relevant piece of information—and then modify your present offer in an appropriate way. This technique gives you a reason to stop at your counterparts' new position rather than at a higher or lower level, and it induces them to question whether their own positions are still valid or need to be reevaluated in light of the new disclosures that have just been made.

When a concession is made in an unplanned manner, it signals anxiety and a loss of control. This is especially true when a position change is made in a tentative and unprincipled fashion by a person who continues to talk nervously and defensively after making the concession. Such behavior suggests a lack of confidence and lets the other side know that the person who has just changed positions does not expect immediate reciprocity. When you encounter such concession-makers, subtly encourage them to keep talking, because this approach will usually generate further unanswered concessions. If you can induce counterparts to bid against themselves through consecutive position changes, you should be able to seize control of the interaction and obtain beneficial results for yourself.

As soon as the concession is announced, you should become quiet and look to your counterpart for an appropriate response. If none is immediately forthcoming, patiently wait for the receiving party to continue the interchange. This lets him or her know that you do not plan further action until your initial movement has been reciprocated.

Carefully Time Your Concessions

The timing of concessions is critical. If you move too quickly, you seem over-eager, and opponents will consider this a sign of weakness. If you make consecutive concessions—or overly generous concessions—you similarly exude weakness. You must remain patient and not move too quickly. You should be certain your opponents reciprocate your position changes to avoid bidding against yourself. On the other hand, persons who are hesitant to make concessions when position changes are expected are likely to anger their counterparts and cause them to think that further talks would not be productive. Such inaction might thus disrupt the entire bargaining interaction.

Plan the Size of Your Concessions

Plan the size of each concession. As you progress in talks, each successive concession should be smaller than the previous one. This will indicate that you are getting closer to your bottom line. When a negotiator makes a concession that is more substantial than his or her prior position changes, this suggests a lack of control that skilled counterparts will try to exploit. Each concession will usually be made in response to an appropriate counteroffer from the other side, but not in an anxious or hurried manner. So take the time to carefully consider your counterpart's concessions, using objective criteria, before announcing another position change of your own.

Let's consider a discussion between a car buyer who hopes to purchase a particular new car for about $23,500. The vehicle has a MSRP (manufacturer's suggested retail price) of $27,000, but it is late in the model year. The prospective purchaser knows that the dealer cost for the car was initially about $24,000, but has learned that the manufacturer has provided dealers with at least a $1,000 rebate. The dealer "holdback" (the amount the dealer will be able to retain if the vehicle is sold within a limited time, often 90 days) is 3 percent (.03 of $24,000 is $720). If the dealer meets this month's sales incentives, he or she will get an additional $500 from the manufacturer. The dealer-buyer discussion might go something like this:

DEALER: You have selected a great automobile; one of our most popular models.

It has a great reputation for quality and safety, and is one of the best-selling cars in the country. The MSRP is $27,000. In addition, a $400 transportation cost, a $150 dealer prep, and a $250 processing fee result in a total of $27,800.

BUYER: I've gotten some information from the Edmunds car-buying service. (See chapter 10 pertaining to car buying.) Your cost for this car was initially $24,000. I know that the manufacturer has provided you with a $1,000 to $1,500 dealer rebate and that you have a 3 percent holdback. If you sell the car now, you should get a manufacturer incentive payment of several hundred dollars. I am willing to include the $400 transportation cost, but am unwilling to pay the $150 dealer prep and the $250 processing fee since they are simply profit enhancers for the dealer. I am willing to give you the incentive as profit and begin the discussions with an offer of $22,180. That includes $24,000 initial cost + $400 transportation cost - $1,500 estimated manufacturer rebate - $720 (3 percent holdback).

DEALER: I can appreciate what a sophisticated car buyer you are. It is always a pleasure to deal with a knowledgeable person, but I must note that your estimate of the manufacturer's rebate is high. It is well below the $1,500 figure you cited.

Furthermore, since it is late in the model year and these cars have been on our lot for several months, we are no longer eligible for the holdback you mentioned.

Nonetheless, I would be in a position to reduce the $27,800 figure by a $2,000 dealer sales incentive and by our $1,000 manufacturer rebate. While I can waive the $150 dealer prep, I must include the $400 transportation cost and the $250 processing fee. This leaves you with a great price of $24,650.

BUYER: I am willing to correct my offer in light of the $1,000 manufacturer rebate, resulting in a figure of $22,680.

DEALER: Based on our end-of-the-month sales incentives, I could come down by another $500 to $24,150. You should appreciate the fact that the specific car you have been considering comes with floor and trunk mats that list for $250 and with mudguards that list for $135.

BUYER: Your actual cost for the mats is only $150 and for the mudguards is $100. I would thus be willing to increase my offer by $250 to $22,930.

DEALER: We have a great deal on our top-of-the-line CD/cassette player. They list for $550, but I could include it in the deal for the $24,150 price.

BUYER: While I would be satisfied with the factory-installed radio, I would not mind the CD/cassette capabilities. I know that your cost for this player is $400. I am thus willing to give you $23,330.

DEALER: I think I could get the sales manager to come down several hundred dollars if we could finalize the deal today. I believe I could get him down to $23,650, but I don't think he would go below that figure.

BUYER: That seems to be a fair price. If you include the CD/cassette player, I would be willing to accept that price.

It is important to note the principled explanations given by the buyer and the dealer for their initial offers and for each successive position change. When each new offer was made, it was accompanied by a rational explanation. The concessions got smaller until the parties reached their agreement. When the parties began to approach an impasse, the dealer avoided a possible deadlock by offering to include the CD/cassette player. The inclusion of this player expanded the pie and allowed the buyer to come up to the dealer's preferred price in a face-saving manner. Furthermore, the dealer cost for the CD/cassette player may have been the $400 figure cited by the buyer, and the dealer could presumably have used the replaced factory-installed radio in another vehicle, thus saving a couple of hundred extra dollars. Through their bargaining exchange, the buyer was able to get the car for a beneficial price, and the dealer was able to make a few hundred dollars on the sale of an end-of-the-year model. This would be a win-win transaction for both participants.

The use of principled concessions allows negotiators to counteract a tendency of their counterparts to devalue the amount of movement involved. They assume that if their adversaries are willing to concede the terms in question, those items must not be of significance to those participants. By indicating why particular concessions are made, those making the offer explain the true value of those changes. This reduces the likelihood the concession recipients will misinterpret the moves and undervalue those position changes.

The aforementioned buyer-dealer negotiation shows how useful it is to plan your anticipated concession patterns in advance. If you initially determine the areas in which you are willing to make concessions, and have your explanations already developed, it will be easier for you to make persuasive position changes. But you cannot plan everything. Since counterparts do not always react as expected, you must be willing to alter your behavior as you learn more about their strengths, weaknesses, and preferences. You must be ready to modify your aspiration level, when appropriate, and also be prepared to alter your concession strategy accordingly.

Be patient during the Distributive Stage. Bargaining interactions take time to complete. When concessions are small and a number of issues must be resolved, allow the process to unfold slowly. Your patience increases the likelihood of agreement and may generate more beneficial results for you. If you attempt to rush the process, the objectivity and the rational criteria you have expressed will lose out to emotional position changes.

Always Remember Your Own and Your Counterpart's Non-Settlement Alternatives

When you enter the Distributive Stage, you must be prepared to make a final offer to your counterparts that would be likely to produce a final agreement. That entails appreciating the non-settlement options available to them and contemplating a final offer that should appeal to reasonably risk-averse opponents. If your final offer is not as appealing as the alternatives available to them, they will reject your offer with confidence. On the other hand, if your final offer is even just slightly better than the other side's external options, they would probably accept it over the uncertainty associated with non-agreement.

Throughout the Distributive Stage, be sure to remember your *own* non-settlement options. You should recognize that it would be irrational to accept proposed terms that are worse than your external alternatives. Keep in mind that as the Distributive Stage evolves and you approach your bottom line, you may feel greater pressure to reach agreement. It is important to realize that when your opponents offer terms that are not much better than what would happen if you reached no agreement, you actually have more—not less—bargaining power. Since there is minimal difference between what you are being offered and what you would have if no deal were achieved, you have little to lose by holding out for better terms.

Don't be afraid to reject marginal offers. Always remember that as you are approaching your bottom line, your counterparts are most likely doing well. Rarely is the settlement range so narrow that both sides must move toward their respective bottom lines in order to reach an agreement. Therefore, in this situation it is likely that your opponents have more to lose from non-settlement than you would. This means that you actually possess greater bargaining power and can afford to demand further opponent concessions as a prerequisite to any agreement.

DEALING WITH IMPASSES AND BARGAINING CONFLICTS

As the Distributive Stage develops, you and your negotiating counterpart may reach temporary impasses. If your non-settlement options are better than what is on the table at that moment, do not hesitate to disclose—at least minimally—the alternatives you have. The more your counterparts appreciate the external options available to you, the more they are likely to move in your direction. Don't convey this information about non-settlement alternatives in a confrontational manner, but rather in a calm and non-confrontational way that is most likely to influence opponent behavior.

A cooperative or an innovative approach is more likely to generate beneficial results than an adversarial strategy. The former styles allow participants to explore the opportunities for mutual gain in a detached win-win manner, while the latter win-lose approach is likely to generate mistrust and create difficulties.

When you are facing stereotypical adversarial opponents who seek win-lose results, try to avoid the seemingly natural quid pro quo response. If both parties behave in an adversarial fashion, the process will break down. Explore the relevant circumstances patiently and calmly. Do not focus on the areas of conflict; instead, explore the areas of overlap. As you succeed in finding areas of mutual gain, both sides will become psychologically committed to settlement.

If specific offers are met with wholly unreceptive replies, use your questioning skills to direct the attention of your opponents back to their underlying needs and interests, and don't hesitate to divulge some of the facts concerning your own goals. The following exchange between a book publisher and a literary agent indicates the way in which cooperative and innovative bargainers can use probing questions to modify the negative mind-sets of adversarial counterparts.

COOPERATIVE PARTY: I gather that you are dissatisfied with our marketing plan?

ADVERSARIAL PARTY: You're damn right I am!

COOPERATIVE PARTY: Please tell me. You are most concerned about the fact my offer doesn't go far enough with respect to promoting your book?

ADVERSARIAL PARTY: That's right. If there is going to be an agreement, you must be willing to make me whole on the issue of national print advertising. You guaranteed it in our contract.

COOPERATIVE PARTY: I assume that if we cannot get space in the Sunday *New York Times Book Review,* you might be able to live with an alternative, such as ads in the *Wall Street Journal?*

ADVERSARIAL PARTY: That is something I could seriously consider.

COOPERATIVE PARTY: I think I could make that happen. How about if I were to run ads for a whole week in the *Journal?*

ADVERSARIAL PARTY: That would be a real improvement over where we began this conversation. Now, is there some way you might be able to address the issue of tour bookings?

Through the use of such non-confrontational inquiries, Cooperators and Innovators can induce Adversaries to replace their unreceptive attitudes with problem-solving views. This transformation contributes greatly to the negotiation process.

On some occasions, despite their best efforts, negotiators approach a stalemate. Before you break off talks and give up, try to explore several other options. If you have been focusing too intently on items causing the impasse, you might shift your discussion to other less conflicted terms that may be amicably resolved. By looking for areas of agreement, you may be able to diminish the significance of your areas of disagreement. You should step back and try to explore unconsidered alternatives that may prove mutually beneficial.

When discussions become tense and heated, it can be productive for the participants to take a short time-out. Recess the talks briefly to reconsider your respective positions, or just change the focus of your discussions for a few minutes to allow everyone to calm down. Talk about local news, sports, mutual acquaintances, or other extraneous topics. Recounting a humorous story can be a good tension reliever, but only if the storyteller has a good sense of humor. If someone lacking a sense of humor tries to lighten things up with a funny story, it may backfire and have the opposite impact.

After several tries, you and your counterparts may still be unable to agree upon the specific issues to be resolved. Perhaps each side still defines the issues in a one-sided manner. Try to step back and look for new ways to present the issues. If the other side has stated a particular issue in an emotionally biased way, try to reframe that issue in a less emotional fashion that you find more acceptable. For example, if someone asks, "How much are you going to pay me for the way you destroyed my storefront?" you can reframe this to "How can I compensate you for the damage I accidentally caused to your storefront?"

You may need to modify your negotiating environment. Try rearranging the furniture into a less confrontational and more pleasant configuration. Or relocate, either to another room in the present building or to another venue entirely. Sometimes the personalities of certain people become a problem. If the participants reach this conclusion, consider bringing in replacements for the remainder of the negotiations.

On some occasions, the best course of action may be to recess talks to allow the parties to calm down and reevaluate their current positions. Before you conclude your present discussions, however, you should agree upon a future meeting date to ensure a continuation of the bargaining process. This will prevent the process from breaking down entirely because of anyone's hesitance to contact the other once talks have broken off.

AUCTION FEVER

When I teach my Negotiation course or make presentations on negotiating to lawyers or businesspeople, I auction off a $1.00 bill—but I have a critical rule that differs from usual auctions. While the highest bidder gets the dollar in exchange for their bid, the second highest bidder does not get the dollar but must still pay me their last bid! I initially elicit a bid of $0.50. Offers are thereafter made in rapid succession of $0.60, $0.70, $0.80, and even $0.90. Someone always bids $0.95, thinking that no rational participant would offer more. What this bidder forgets is that the second highest bidder is required to pay me their last bid even though they don't get any money. When the second highest bidder hears the $0.95 bid, they can easily be coaxed into a bid of $1.00 to guarantee a break-even result.

Once the $1.00 bid has been made, the auction comes to a temporary halt. The bidders and the observers are shocked by the developments that have occurred. I then remind the person at $0.95 that he or she can reduce the overall loss to $0.05 with a bid of $1.05. I always generate a $1.05 bid. The person who thought they had prevailed at $1.00 usually bids $1.10 and the bidding continues to $1.50, $1.75, or $2.00. At this point, one of the bidders is likely to recognize the losing venture in which they are involved, and stop bidding. Nonetheless, on several occasions I have generated bids of $2.50 to $3.00. Once, in my Negotiation class, I got a final bid of $20.00! I was shocked by the fact the $20.00 bidder thought he had "won."

The purpose of this seemingly frivolous "dollar auction" is to demonstrate how easily bidders can become *psychologically entrapped* by the process itself. Bidders initially think they will make some easy money. They quickly discover, however, that they must accept a loss. They are especially unhappy with the fact the other bidder is going to "beat" them, thus they continue beyond any rational stopping point. While they know they are going to lose money, it now becomes important to be certain they don't "lose" to the other bidder. They would prefer to pay me more money than to have the other party "prevail."

Know When to Walk Away

The entrapment factor at auctions is generated by the bidding frenzy and the fact that each bidder wants to "win" by outbidding the others. Less reputable auction houses may even have shills bidding on items in an effort to drive up the prices. If you are a serious auction-goer, you do your homework ahead of time and determine what you would have to pay elsewhere for the items being offered. When the bidding gets too high, intelligent bidders withdraw. On the other hand, entrapped bidders continue until they experience "winner's curse" by obtaining items at prices well above their actual value.

Don't ever allow yourself to become so caught up in the bargaining "game" that you find yourself compelled to achieve final deals no matter the cost. You must learn to recognize when you have become involved in losing efforts and to know how to minimize your losses. How? Know your non-settlement options before entering the negotiation. What are the best terms you could obtain if you failed to reach an agreement with your counterpart? If you have established this, you will know when to walk away and accept your non-settlement alternatives.

The psychological entrapment experienced by negotiators is generated by the substantial amount of time and effort they have put into the bargaining process. Careless participants are afraid to allow these efforts to be wasted through negotiation "failures," and they continue to seek deals that are objectively worse than their non-settlement alternatives. Your negotiation efforts rarely are in vain. You had to negotiate to ascertain whether this course would produce results preferable to your non-settlement options. You now have important information that you should accept your external alternatives. Had you not engaged in the bargaining process, you would not be confident that you should choose your non-settlement options.

When you prepare for negotiations, carefully examine your non-settlement alternatives. Know what you could accomplish through other avenues. When it becomes clear that you can't achieve preferable terms through the bargaining process, politely terminate the interaction. When you calmly explain to your opponents that you can achieve better results through other avenues, they may decide to offer you more generous terms. If they fail to do so, you can confidently choose your non-settlement options.

Never continue the bargaining encounter merely because of the amount of time and effort you have already expended. Never attempt to "beat" your opponents by increasing your offers above the actual value of the items being exchanged. Never be afraid to accept the consequences associated with non-settlements, when those consequences are clearly preferable to what you can achieve through the negotiation process. If you continue to negotiate once you realize that you are involved in a losing effort, you will regret the final results.

Classic examples of bargaining entrapment occur when individuals look for new houses, new jobs, and even new romantic partners. Individuals make offers on several houses they would like to purchase, only to have those bids rejected. After they have lost several houses they desire, they bid on a house they don't particularly like. Their offer is accepted, and they are stuck with a dwelling they don't really want. After losing several preferable houses, they wanted to obtain a "win." To accomplish this goal, they made an offer on a less desirable property and got stuck with it.

Individuals seeking different employment opportunities or new romantic partners often experience similar entrapment. They are rejected by several business firms or desirable mates. They become tired of losing, and they seek a "victory" when they locate a less desirable position or a person they don't love. Next thing they know, they have accepted the less preferable employment situation or have moved in with this new dating partner. This is why people who have recently lost good jobs or have broken up with significant others must be careful not to seize the next employment opportunity or fall for someone else on the rebound. Ask yourselves what employment opportunities you really desire and what individuals you would truly like to be with. If no one or nothing suitable becomes available in the immediate future, be patient. If you fail to recognize the psychological entrapment you fall into, you are almost certain to experience the dreaded "winner's curse."

POWER BARGAINING TACTICS

Despite faithful use of principled positions, objective criteria, and carefully applied concession strategy, you may need to use bargaining tactics to help things along. During your preparation, determine what tactics would be most effective against your particular counterparts in light of the specific issues involved. Use them in isolation or in combination, and try to vary your approaches to keep counterparts off balance. Adopt only the techniques that suit your own personality. The most important ones to have in your repertoire are factual, economic, and emotional arguments.

Factual, Economic, and Emotional Arguments

At some point during almost every negotiation, the participants argue for their preferred positions. Some make detached analytical arguments, while others make emotional appeals. Each can be effective, depending on the individuals and circumstances involved.

If analytical arguments of a factual or economic nature are to be persuasive, they must be presented in a sufficiently neutral manner that they are taken seriously. Wholly one-sided presentations are too easily dismissed as self-serving. In addition, persuasive arguments go beyond the expected, forcing opponents to reconsider their own assumptions and positions in a way that works to the benefit of those articulating the arguments.

For instance, when the underlying facts militate in favor of the claims you are advancing, focus on the most relevant factual circumstances. Compel your opponents to grasp the importance of this information. If you present these details effectively, by the time you have laid them out, your counterparts will be predisposed toward your claims. For example, if I am representing an individual who has been injured in an automobile accident, I might go over the actual injuries and necessary medical treatment in great detail. I want the listener to "feel" the pain my client experienced. I want them to appreciate the medical expenses my client has incurred. This makes it difficult for them to deny the significance of my client's injuries and enhances the likelihood they will make a realistic opening offer to compensate my client for the pain and suffering involved.

The same can be said of good economic assertions. When the economic circumstances favor your situation, describe these pieces of information in a detached and detailed manner. Make it difficult for opponents to refute your contentions. If you are buying or selling a house or car, it helps immeasurably to obtain objective information you can use to guide the discussions. What have similar houses in the area sold for over the past few months? What is the retail value of vehicles in comparison to the one being bought or sold? If you are the prospective owner, focus on the lower price range for houses or cars; if you are the prospective seller, focus on the upper range.

Some negotiators are afraid to make emotional appeals, in the belief that they are inappropriate during professional discussions. This is not true. Not only are they appropriate, but they are extremely effective. If you are fortunate enough to make presentations that provide you with irrefutable moral support, don't lose the opportunity. This is caused by the guilt generated in adversaries by effective emotional appeals. Studies show that highly intelligent people are more likely to succumb to good emotional contentions than to purely abstract claims, because they find it difficult to counter the emotional presentations.[1]

When your counterparts present their arguments, it is important that you recognize these as one-sided appeals. They are disclosing the information that best supports their positions, and you must try to ascertain the issues they have not addressed. What facts have they omitted from their factual claims? What economic data have they left out of their economic analysis? Has their moral appeal ignored circumstances that may either undermine their claim or bolster your position? During negotiation discussions, participants try to put the best face on their positions. Your counterparts will surely do so with you.

In fact, anticipate opponent arguments while you're preparing your arguments, and formulate cogent counter-arguments. When you prepare your own arguments and counter-arguments, be certain not to become so enamored with your assertions that you convince yourself completely of your right to prevail on every issue. You must keep your objectivity. If you don't, and you are unable to appreciate the valid claims of your opponents, you may find it difficult to make the concessions during the process that will make mutual accords possible.

Threats, Warnings, and Promises

During negotiations, you and your counterparts are likely to resort to express or implicit threats. Each party informs the other that if it does not give in on certain points, dire consequences will follow. For example, "If you don't give me a raise, I'll leave the firm."

The purpose of a threat is to convince the other side that their non-settlement alternatives are worse than your demands. If you are contemplating making a threat, construct it as follows:

1. Be sure the negative consequences are sufficiently realistic so your opponents will believe them.

2. Convey enough information to clearly communicate the negative impact of a non-settlement and the threatened consequences, and make the negative effects sufficiently serious so they appear worse than giving in to your demands.

3. Be prepared to carry out the consequences. If you threaten someone and back down when they call your bluff, your credibility is destroyed.

There are *threats* and there are *warnings*. A warning is a sanction that will be imposed by a third party or by the marketplace. For example, "If you don't reduce the rent you are seeking, you will be unable to rent your space" (that is, no one will pay that amount). If an individual is angry with a neighbor who sawed down a tree on his side of the property line, a "warning" would be the consequences the court would impose if the offending party does not rectify the situation promptly. A threat involves negative consequences the threatening party will himself impose. For example: "If you don't replace the tree you cut down, I will sue you."

If possible, state the negative consequences of non-settlements as "warnings" rather than "threats." Nobody likes to be threatened. Also, when you personally threaten to punish opponents, they reflexively want to call your bluff. On the other hand, when you "predict" what third parties or the marketplace will do if adversaries do not accept your terms, this softens the negative impact since you are merely indicating what some other force will do. You also enhance believability since the external factor you are discussing is beyond your control.

When you receive a threat, consider two critical factors:

1. Do you believe your counterpart will carry out his or her threat? If your answer is yes, then ask yourself:

2. Would the consequences of that threat be worse than your non-settlement alternatives?

If you know that you would be better off refusing to give in to the threat, feel free to ignore it. It is usually advantageous not to directly challenge the threat since this may induce your counterpart to carry it out. If you merely ignore the threat and act as if you are unaware of it, the counterpart may decide to continue the discussions as if he or she had never made the threat. This allows you to neutralize the threatened conduct in a face-saving manner.

At the other end of the spectrum from threats and warnings are *promises*. A promise does not involve the suggestion of negative consequences, but rather consists of a commitment to reward the other side if it behaves appropriately. For example, you have purchased reconditioned office supplies for your company from a broker. The twenty-five chairs you ordered have just been delivered and five are the wrong model. Here is your phone conversation:

YOU: Twenty percent of the delivery we received today is the wrong model.

BROKER: The seller only had twenty of the chairs you wanted so I had him substitute a higher-priced model to fill out the order.

YOU: Those chairs are not what I ordered, and they don't fit our needs. I'm not paying for them. Get someone to pick them up.

BROKER: Our contract explicitly states that comparable substitutions can be made if I can't locate an item.

YOU: I'm not happy with the way you executed this deal, and I'm not paying for one chair. I'm arranging for the entire shipment to be waiting at the warehouse entrance first thing tomorrow morning for your guys to pick up.

BROKER: I'm sorry you're not satisfied. If you will agree to send back just the five chairs, I will give you a full refund on them.

YOU: All right.

As demonstrated above, instead of threatening to punish opponents who do not modify their position, you can indicate a willingness to change your own position if they alter their position. You thus promise to *reward* affirmative behavior instead of *punishing* negative behavior.

The Intelligent Negotiator gets a lot more mileage out of promises than the more offensive threats or warnings. However, the principal reason promises are more effective is that they are face-saving. The greatest fear negotiators have when they modify their existing positions is that their position changes will not be reciprocated. When you promise to change your offer if they change theirs, you alleviate this concern.

Most negotiators frequently use the promise device as they reach the end of their bargaining interactions. If you and your counterpart are not far apart, one side may suggest that you conclude your talks by splitting the distance. How much nicer it is to say "If you'll go halfway, I will too," rather than "If you don't go halfway, the whole deal is off." Instead of using a threat or warning when an earlier impasse is looming, simply indicate your willingness to modify your current position if your opponent is willing to alter his or her position. This will probably generate new positions that are closer together and will keep the discussions going.

Humor

Humor can be used both as a negative and a positive force during negotiations. It can increase the likability of the person using the humor. Individuals should not hesitate to use their sense of humor during the preliminary discussions to develop more open and trusting relationships with counterparts. If you can become more likable to your counterparts, it will be more difficult for those persons to reject your offers.

Humor can also be used during tense negotiations to relieve anxiety and to reopen blocked communication channels. I recall the story of unusually acrimonious labor negotiations between a large union and a group of employers. After an impasse had been reached, the parties stared intently at one another across the bargaining table. The chief negotiator from the union arose from his seat and began to walk slowly around the table toward the employer side. The room became completely silent by the time he arrived next to the chief negotiator for the employers. He squatted beside that individual and looked at his union colleagues on the other side of the table. When he said, "From here, you guys *do* look like sons of bitches," everyone laughed and much of the prevailing tension was broken. He used his sense of humor to point out to both sides that the representatives of each side were merely performing their jobs. By depersonalizing the conflict, he was able to get the participants back on track.

Humor can be used during bargaining encounters to soften the impact of negative statements. When you feel the need to say something negative, say it with a slight smile. This may make it easier for your listeners to accept the criticism. Since they are not sure you meant to sound so negative, they don't take your comments as personally as they would if they were not accompanied by a smile.

When counterparts announce wholly unacceptable opening positions, you may respond with a sneer or derisive laughter. Your behavior ridicules their stance and indicates rather directly the unreasonableness of the proposed terms. The use of such ridicule is risky because it can easily offend the targets. If you have a good sense of humor, you may be able to soften the ridicule with the twinkle in your eye. If, however, you use derisive humor with a completely straight face, your recipients will perceive it far more negatively.

Control of Bargaining Agenda

Many skilled negotiators try to advance their objectives through control of the bargaining agenda. You can do this in several ways. You can present a written agenda at the onset of discussions, or you can verbally do the following: Lay out your opening offers in a principled manner in which you mention each component and provide a rationale to support each claim, thus defining the issues you wish to address. Less prepared counterparts may accept your definition of the pertinent items and address the terms as you have broken them down.

The value of having your counterparts follow the order you have provided is that it enables you to have the items you value resolved first—before the other issues are addressed. Once these have been taken care of to your satisfaction, you may find it easier to be more accommodating when your counterparts raise other items.

If your counterparts create the agenda and you don't like it, don't hesitate to say something. This is an appropriate time to set the ground rules for the way in which the various terms are to be explored. If you and your counterparts can agree upon the order to be used to address the different items, you'll have established a positive bargaining environment that will benefit you when they become involved with the substantive trades.

Intransigence

Successful negotiators are able at critical points to convince their opponents that those individuals must make appropriate concessions if the process is to continue. This may be accomplished though sheer intransigence. Intransigence can be especially effective when used against risk-averse people who fear the negative consequences of non-settlements.

For example, an employer offering a person a new job may offer that person a $50,000 salary. When the applicant responds that she is contemplating something in the $60,000 range, the employer may simply reiterate the $50,000 figure, indicate that $50,000 is the salary for this position, and become silent. If the applicant is anxious to get the position in question, she may quickly accede to the intransigent offer of the employer.

Keep in mind that this tactic is only effective with counterparts whose options are no better than what you are offering.

Directness

Most professional negotiators see a significant amount of disingenuous behavior during bargaining encounters, all of it designed to manipulate their behavior. They may be disarmed by individuals who say what they are really thinking. Try to surprise opponents with your candor. On several occasions when opposing lawyers have threatened to sue my clients, I have accepted their initial factual and legal assertions then asked them to indicate what they would consider a fair resolution of the dispute. They have been so surprised when I did not contest everything they said that they changed their demands to be more realistic, allowing us to begin exploring settlement options in more positive negotiating environments.

Flattery

Showing your counterparts that you respect them may cause them to become more accommodating at the bargaining table. We all like to be appreciated. People who feel esteemed by their opponents may not feel the same need to demonstrate their bargaining prowess as they would to less respectful adversaries. At the very least, flattery will create a more positive bargaining atmosphere and help the interaction progress more smoothly. For instance, you can acknowledge your counterpart's notable contributions to a field of mutual endeavor, show admiration for a recent victory he or she has achieved, or compliment the design of his or her office environment.

Manipulation of Contextual Factors

Some individuals attempt to gain a psychological advantage during bargaining interactions through their manipulation of the contextual factors—the date, time, location, and environment for the discussions. Many people feel most comfortable meeting in their own room or office. They also like to set the early tone by controlling the date and time for the talks. People who induce counterparts to meet at their preferred location or time may place those counterparts in a concessionary frame of mind that will carry over to the substantive bargaining.

If you can induce opponents to meet at your office, this may also allow you to generate feelings of obligation by providing them with food and drink. While you may question whether such insignificant gratuities would be likely to influence anyone, I prefer to be the provider rather than the recipient of such generosity. If you doubt the impact of these gestures, take the time to observe religious solicitors who operate in airports or train stations. They initiate their interactions by providing little flowers or other small gifts. They then attempt to establish rapport through casual touching and sincere eye contact. It is amazing to see how quickly people who decline to make contributions try to return the flowers or other gifts they have received!

Silence

Silence is one of the most effective—yet overlooked—bargaining techniques. Less experienced negotiators often don't realize the power of silence. They are afraid they will lose control of the interaction if they stop talking. When they encounter prolonged pauses, they feel compelled to speak. When they do so, they disclose information they did not plan to divulge, and they often make unplanned concessions.

Impatient opponents often continue to explain their positions in response to your prolonged silence and make further position changes because of the discomfort they are experiencing. By inducing them to bid against themselves with consecutive opening offers or unreciprocated concessions, you can generate repeated opponent movement that you do not have to match.

When you have something important to say, try to convey your message succinctly then become quiet. If you reiterate what you just said, you look uncertain, may disclose additional information, and may make unintended concessions. Silence is thus especially important after you have made your opening offer and following each position change. Once your position statements have been made, it is the other side's turn to respond. By your silence, you signal to them their need to continue the process with their own communication.

When you encounter taciturn opponents, don't assume personal responsibility to keep the discussions going. Say what you have to say in a concise manner and become quiet. Again, it is your opponent's turn to speak. If he or she doesn't respond, wait patiently. If a minute or two goes by without any conversation, the time may seem like an eternity. Don't allow your discomfort to induce you to speak inappropriately. If you wait long enough, such adversaries will almost always recognize their need to talk if the process is to continue. What should you do if they refuse to speak for four or five minutes? Ask whether they are planning a response to what you just said. Such a question places the onus on them to talk. Or get up and head for the exit. If they remain silent, you should go home or return to your office. If they ask where you are going, you can indicate you are leaving because of their unwillingness to respond to your prior offer. This is a prime example of *attitudinal bargaining.*

Patience

Patience is as powerful a bargaining tool as silence. We Americans are known around the world for our talkative nature and our impatience. This is especially true during bargaining encounters. Negotiators from more patient cultures wait calmly—and often quietly—for us to fill the silent voids with new information and concessions. The negotiation process takes time to develop. This is especially true when parties are attempting to resolve conflicts that have created strong emotions. It takes time for most people to move from a combative stance to a more conciliatory mode. If you attempt to rush the process, adversaries may become even angrier. If, on the other hand, you patiently await developments and exude a willingness to reason together for as long as it takes to achieve mutually beneficial accords, you enhance the likelihood of successful interactions.

When opponents give you specific time frames, don't always expect them to honor those deadlines. They may promise a response to your last offer by the beginning of next week—but fail to get back to you by next Tuesday. This may be an inadvertent oversight on their part—or it may be a deliberate tactic designed to increase your anxiety level. Try not to call them next Tuesday or Wednesday to ask what they are thinking. Double their time frame and patiently await their belated response. They will usually call you by Thursday or Friday, wondering why you have not yet contacted them. If you calmly reply that you assumed they were busy and knew they would contact you as soon as they could, this will unnerve them. They had hoped to use time pressure to disconcert you, and you have demonstrated that this tactic will not work.

Guilt or Embarrassment

In his classic book *When I Say No, I Feel Guilty,*[2] Manuel J. Smith described the degree to which children can generate parental guilt to obtain concessions during bargaining en-

counters. The children make seemingly unreasonable requests they know their responsible parents must reject.
When the parents begin to feel guilty, the children offer
less outrageous alternatives that the parents feel obliged
to accept. I know two attorney-parents who were discussing the negotiation process in front of their young
daughter. They didn't realize how closely she was listening
to their conversation, until she responded to one of their
comments regarding the need for exaggerated opening positions. She said: "Is that like when I ask you to have two
or three friends sleep over when I really only want one?"

When you think that opponents have asserted unrealistic positions, don't hesitate to make them feel guilty by
calmly explaining how unreasonable those positions are.
If counterparts show up late or engage in other inappropriate behavior, don't hesitate to exploit their embarrassment to generate greater concessions from them. You don't
have to say much—just enough to cause them discomfort.
Simply mention how long you have been waiting for them
or how personally offended you are by their sarcastic comment. If you then wait silently and patiently, they will
usually reward you with further position changes.

Never gloat when counterparts make concessions.
Accept their position changes graciously, and let them
know how much you appreciate their reasonableness. As
you near the conclusion of a bargaining encounter, remember to leave your counterparts with the sense that
they got a good deal. You can accomplish this objective by
making one or two minor concessions as you conclude
your interaction. If they suspect they have been cleaned
out, opponents may experience "buyer's remorse" and try
to get out of the agreement. Even if they are unable to escape the present deal, they will be out for blood the next
time they have to interact with you.

Let's see the way Felicia handles the distributive stage of her job negotiations with Andersen.

Felicia informs Solomon that Andersen's health coverage and pension plan are acceptable. She expects a higher salary, more than two weeks of vacation, and the right to take relevant training courses at firm expense. Solomon quickly indicates a willingness to provide her with a $60,000 salary and with three weeks of vacation. He acknowledges the changing nature of the technology field and suggests that Andersen would be willing to pay "several thousand dollars" each year for computer courses, if Felicia promises not to allow her time at these classes to adversely affect her work. She says that she would work nights and weekends, if necessary, to be sure Andersen's networks continue to operate efficiently during her training programs.

Felicia asks Solomon if he has additional flexibility with respect to her salary. She is surprised when he replies that Harry Andersen, the company president, is not inclined to authorize a higher base salary for that position because he is not sure how fast they can expand their e-business. Felicia attempts to circumvent this issue by asking if the firm would agree to provide her with annual bonuses based on the degree to which their e-business is growing. Solomon seems to consider this a fair compromise and suggests a bonus of up to $5,000 based upon annual e-business revenue growth. He says that greater bonuses may be available in future years once the firm's e-business has become established.

Felicia next asks Solomon if he would agree to evaluate her performance in six months and increase her salary if he is satisfied with her work. He says he would be willing to do this and provide her with an increase of up to $2,500 for good performance.

Felicia indicates that she would participate in the firm's stock option plan, and Solomon explains the details of that program. Solomon says that the firm would reimburse her for moving expenses up to a maximum of $3,000. He then offers her a $1,000 signing bonus. Felicia says she appreciates his flexibility with respect to these issues. Both Felicia and Solomon are confident they will achieve a mutual accord.

Solomon finally asks Felicia how soon she can start work. She says she would like to begin in eight weeks to give them time to find a house and relocate. He looks disappointed and wonders if she might be able to start sooner. She promises to discuss this matter with her husband and get back to him.

SUMMARY POINTS

- In the Distributive Stage, the parties divide the items they have discovered in the Information Exchange. This is a highly competitive part of their interaction because it determines what each side gets.

- No matter how much the participants strive for "win-win" results, both sides will want some of the same items, and they will dispute the division of these terms. Because the level of competition is so intense, adapting your style of bargaining accordingly is particularly important.

- Skilled negotiators establish principled opening positions and are guided by objective criteria.

- Because concession strategy is critical, Intelligent Negotiators plan their concession strategies carefully.

- The elements of a successful concession strategy are self-confidence, principled positions, careful planning of size as well as timing of concessions, and always keeping in mind your own and your counterpart's non-settlement options.

- Various bargaining ploys can be useful during the distributive stage. These include arguments, threats, warnings, promises, humor, control of the agenda, intransigence, directness, flattery, manipulation of contextual factors, silence, patience, and creation of guilt.

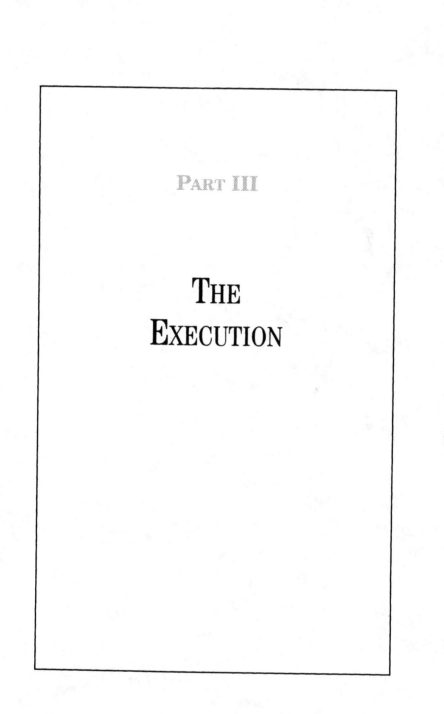

PART III

THE
EXECUTION

CHAPTER 6

NEGOTIATING TECHNIQUES

Skilled negotiators employ various techniques to advance their interests during distributive encounters. Whether you use a cooperative, innovative, or adversarial negotiating style, you will need to employ different techniques along the way to facilitate your bargaining. Since it is impossible to change your true personality to suit a particular technique, select a bargaining style and tactics that are consistent with your natural disposition. When done well, some of these techniques can become natural extensions of the people using them. For example, aggressive people may adopt an aggressive negotiating style, while laid-back individuals may use a calm and deferential approach.

Negotiators use a limited number of techniques during bargaining interactions to enable them to claim what is on the table. If you can identify the bargaining tactics your negotiating counterparts use against you and understand the strengths and weaknesses associated with each tactic, you can effectively neutralize their negative impact. This will enhance your bargaining confidence. It also helps you determine what tactics you should employ to advance your own interests during particular bargaining encounters.

BARGAINING ALONE AGAINST SEVERAL COUNTERPARTS

Most bargaining interactions are conducted on a one-on-one basis in person or on the telephone. In some situations, especially those of a commercial nature, participants try to obtain a psychological advantage by teaming up against a single opponent. They hope to use the extra person(s) to intimidate their lone adversary and to help them listen for verbal leaks and watch for nonverbal signals emanating from their opponent. They also believe that the excessive verbal and nonverbal stimuli emanating from the different members of their bargaining team will overwhelm a lone opponent who has to watch, listen, think, and speak simultaneously. Car dealers often employ this tactic when the discussions between the salesperson and the customer become serious. The sales manager may then be brought in as an extra participant. Many real estate brokers also use this ploy by working in teams of two or three.

When you are forced to negotiate alone against two or three counterparts, you almost always lose! Why? It is virtually impossible for a single individual to out-think, out-hear, out-watch, and out-perform several well-coordinated opponents. When lone participants are talking, they tend to concentrate so much on what they are saying that they miss the nonverbal signals emanating from their counterparts and themselves. When one member of the opposing bargaining team is speaking, the lone negotiator finds it difficult to listen intently to the speaker and to look for nonverbal clues being emitted by other team members. When the participants take a break, multi-party team members are able to meet with the members of their own negotiating group to determine how things are going and to compare notes with each other while the lone negotiator has no one to consult.

In my law school Negotiation class, some of the exercises are conducted on a one-on-one basis, while others are done on a two-on-two basis. When the students are assigned partners, there are occasions when one partner is ill or out of town and unable to participate. When this happens, the single negotiator has to interact with two counterparts. In almost all cases, the lone bargainer finishes near the bottom of the class. Almost never does the single participant obtain results that are above average.

When you have to engage in bargaining encounters with several people on the other side, take someone else with you. Depending on the circumstances, this person might be a friend, a spouse, a coworker, a parent, or an adult child. This is especially important when you are involved in discussions with professional negotiators whom you have good reason to believe have deliberately expanded their bargaining groups to place you on the defensive. The addition of just one negotiator diminishes the advantage that counterparts derive from a larger bargaining team. Your partner can monitor the verbal messages and nonverbal signals while you more actively interact with the various counterparts.

Some negotiators who add a person to their bargaining teams use that individual as a "silent partner." They ask him or her not to speak, except in extraordinary circumstances. This can be effective. By just having the extra person present, the team negates the advantage multi-party counterparts are trying to obtain. It is usually preferable, however, to take someone with you who can at least minimally participate. He or she may see an opening that you have missed. If the extra person is unable to speak immediately, the opportunity may be lost; whereas by jumping right in to exploit the opening, he or she can be of great assistance. To enhance the ability of a partner to facilitate the bargaining process, make sure he or she is thoroughly prepared for the interaction. Before you meet with your counterparts, you and your partner must review everything and decide how to proceed. You must be prepared to conduct carefully coordinated talks based on unified goals and a cohesive strategy. If any member of your group does not understand his or her role, the benefit of having a multi-party bargaining team may be lost.

If you work for a large organization, there may be times when a number of people decide to participate in a significant negotiation. Individuals from each department that may be affected by the final result might demand input. During the preparation process, you must conduct a large intra-organizational negotiation in which all interested parties are invited to participate. You must develop a set of common goals and a unified bargaining strategy. If you fail to do this, your counterparts will discover the weak links on your side and exploit them. If ten, fifteen, or twenty persons plan to attend the joint bargaining sessions, you must carefully decide who will address which issues. If everyone on your side is authorized to speak, your counterparts will target your weakest team members and take advantage of those individuals. Designate two or three people who will do all the talking for your side, or divide the issues into groups and indicate the particular individuals who will address each group of items.

TIME PRESSURE

When individuals negotiate, whether in real estate, car, or job transactions, they generally feel time urgency, believing that if they don't act quickly they will be out of luck. But when individuals negotiate in business transactions, they are more likely to understand that moving too quickly gives the other side a significant advantage.

Japanese negotiators frequently use the time factor to advance their interests. When they are visited by foreign corporate representatives who hope to negotiate business deals with Japanese firms, the Japanese hosts ask their visitors about their return flight schedule so they can reconfirm those flights. They then use generous hospitality to preclude the beginning of substantive discussions as they try to become better acquainted with their future business partners. Several days before their visitors are scheduled to fly home, the Japanese negotiators get down to business and obtain substantial concessions from individuals who feel they can't return home empty-handed. Similar tactics are often used by insurance company representatives to settle claims filed by injured people who need financial assistance immediately. If the claimants hired lawyers and filed lawsuits, their cases might not go to trial for several years. Most injured people cannot wait that long to obtain compensation for their injuries, and they settle their claims for far less than they deserve.

If you are ever in a situation where you feel time pressure, try to withhold that information whenever possible. For example, if you are selling your house and are asked by prospective purchasers when you plan to relocate, you may either say that you don't have to move until you have sold your house or state that you plan to rent your home if it is not sold by a certain date. If you are trying to purchase a new home, a selling real estate agent may ask you how soon you plan to move to the new area, hoping to find out how quickly you need to get another house. You can indicate a willingness to rent a place if you don't locate something you like to allow you to become more familiar with the new market.

Negotiators who feel time pressure forget to ask themselves one critical question: How much is the time factor affecting their *counterparts*? In most bargaining situations, *both sides* want to conclude the deal quickly. If you ignore the time pressure influencing your adversaries, you concede this valuable factor to those individuals. Ask yourself how soon *they* want to finish this interaction. They may have a shorter time frame than you have. If they do, you can exude a patience that will cause them to make the concessions that are necessary to conclude the deal by their deadline.

When you have a definite deadline that must be met, you can preempt the time factor. When you first meet with your counterparts, directly inform them of your time limit and indicate that if no agreement is achieved by that date, you will accept your non-settlement alternatives. No matter how much time they may actually have, you are telling them that *your* deadline is *their* deadline. If no deal is reached by then, there will be no deal. Never misrepresent this factor because it would be considered unethical and the risks would be substantial.

Communicating Dual Messages

Some communications contain *dual messages*—one apparently objective and forthright, and the other subtle and ulterior. For example, a real estate seller might openly suggest to a prospective buyer who is thinking of purchasing certain property he or she could barely afford that "you probably can't afford this house." While this overtly "adult"-to-"adult" statement may be objectively accurate, the seller doesn't really wish to convince the prospective buyer of this fact because this would preclude a sale. The ulterior message is conveyed in a "parent"-to-"child" manner, with the "parent"-seller informing the "child"-buyer that he or she can't do something. If the truly desired response is generated, the prospective purchaser will respond with a "child"-like "Yes I can!" Through this manipulative technique, the salesperson may be able to sell a house to someone who was not contemplating such expensive property.

You should be suspicious of opponent statements suggesting that contemplated transactions can't or shouldn't be consummated. If the speakers really believed this fact, they would not be negotiating with you. If, despite such communications, the speakers exhibit a desire to continue the bargaining discussions, it is likely they are disingenuously attempting to entrap you into accepting what are probably disadvantageous arrangements.

EXTREME OPENING OFFERS

I discussed earlier how important it is for negotiators to develop high aspiration levels during your preparation and to plan opening offers that give you sufficient bargaining room. While I noted the need to always demand more or offer less than you hope to obtain, I also emphasized the importance of beginning with an offer you can rationally defend to preserve your credibility. If you don't know how to judge the reasonableness of your opening offers, you might attempt to protect yourself by starting with extreme positions. This is a risky approach, because it may completely turn off counterparts who may give up and do business with someone else. On the other hand, it may work. You could be lucky enough to negotiate with careless counterparts who forget to focus on their own non-settlement options; if you are, your extreme positions may pay off.

When you are confronted with your counterpart's truly outrageous opening offers, don't casually dismiss them by suggesting they may be "a bit high" or "a bit low." Counterparts who begin with extreme positions either know how unreasonable those offers are and expect you to respond appropriately, or they have no idea and need you to enlighten them. If you don't demonstrate complete shock, they begin to think their positions are not really that extreme. They reassess their goals away from reality in a way that decreases the likelihood of final agreements.

As soon as you receive unrealistic opening offers, firmly but politely indicate how unacceptable those positions are. For example, you might say: "You and I know how unrealistic your position is. What you are proposing is entirely unacceptable. If these are the areas you hope to explore, we have nothing to discuss." Once you convey this message to your unrealistic adversaries, they will begin to lower their expectation level without fearing that their preliminary assessment was completely erroneous.

What should you do with counterparts who refuse to veer from their extreme opponent opening offers even after you have indicated your displeasure with those positions? You can indicate an unwillingness to articulate any offer of your own until the other side has placed a reasonable offer on the table. Some negotiators will refuse to bid against themselves in this manner and will restate their original offer. If this happens, you may then offer your own opening position that is as unrealistic as that of the other side. Then use attitudinal bargaining and the *promise* technique and suggest a willingness to provide a more reasonable offer *as soon as* they provide you with a fair offer. "You and I both realize how outrageous our respective positions are. We can continue with these absurd positions and waste a lot of time. Or, if you are willing to put a realistic position on the table, I will respond in kind, and we can begin the serious discussions." This approach often produces beneficial results.

You can ignore the unreasonable nature of your counterparts and announce your own realistic opening offer, hoping to embarrass your adversaries into more accommodating behavior. This is a risky approach because you will quickly find yourself close to where you hope to end up while facing the other side's initial position that is far from that point. You will then have to force your counterparts to make huge concessions in exchange for each of your smaller position changes. It is difficult to sustain this effort. As your counterparts point out how far they have moved compared with your minimal progress, you feel guilty and often give them better terms than they deserve.

PROBING QUESTIONS

A different technique can be especially effective to counter unrealistic opening positions announced by the other side. Instead of arguing with them, take out a pad of paper and indicate how much you would like to understand their position. Break their offer into components— and begin with the more finite items for which it would be difficult to puff credibly. For example, if you are thinking of purchasing someone else's business, you initially ask how they have valued the property involved. If they provide a remotely realistic figure, write it down and go on the next items (such as building and equipment, inventory, accounts receivable, patents and trademarks, and goodwill). If the number they cite is unreasonable, you calmly explain how you recently had the property appraised at $500,000 and ask how they got the $1,500,000 figure. The goal is not to argue with them, but merely to reason together in a highly professional manner. They have most likely had the property appraised recently and know its true value. They will then respond with a slightly exaggerated figure of $700,000. You write this number down and move on to the other items. When you are finished and add up the new total, it is one-fourth or one-fifth of their initial demand.

When people begin with wholly unrealistic opening positions, they have made them up. They have no idea how to defend them in a rational manner. When you break the underlying issues into finite parts and ask them to value each of the parts, opponents can no longer maintain their absurd positions. As they provide direct answers to your specific inquiries, their initial position crumbles and they end up in a more realistic area.

BEST-OFFER-FIRST (TAKE-IT-OR-LEAVE-IT) BARGAINING

You may not like participating in the usual give-and-take of the bargaining process where the parties begin far apart and move toward the center. Perhaps you find such concession-bargaining distasteful, or your bargaining position is powerful enough that you can avoid it. What you can do instead is to determine what you are willing to give to the other side before you initially meet with them. You then arrive at the first bargaining session and announce a firm offer that you are unwilling to modify. If the other side accepts your terms, you have an agreement. If not, there is no accord. From the perspective of the one making the offer, this is known as *best-offer-first* bargaining. From the recipient's perspective, it is called *take-it-or-leave-it* negotiating.

Many insurance company agents use best-offer-first bargaining when they negotiate with claimants. They announce the figures they are willing to recommend to their superiors and indicate a complete unwillingness to modify those terms. They are successful with desperate claimants who need money now and cannot wait until they can obtain effective legal assistance. On the other hand, they are wholly unsuccessful with claimants who are willing to wait until higher insurance firm representatives who are willing to discuss more generous terms become involved.

You often lose out with best-offer-first bargaining for two reasons. One, you have skipped the information exchange. Without that, it is difficult for you to determine the value of what is being negotiated. You need to talk with the other side to ascertain the degree to which that side wants the deal. Your counterparts may be willing to accept less generous terms than you anticipate. The use of best-offer-first bargaining deprives you of any opportunity to do better than your first offer. The second reason you often lose with this technique is that it greatly increases the probability of non-settlements, because of the way in which the recipients of such offers react. These are "parent"-to-"child" interactions. The "parent" gets to determine unilaterally what is good for both sides. They then present their "final" offers to their "child"-like counterparts in a patronizing manner that is likely to be viewed as highly offensive. If the recipients respond in a "child"-like fashion, they may reject even reasonable offers that have been presented in such an insulting way.

Individuals who use the best-offer-first approach normally have a substantial amount of bargaining power. You have to possess a lot of authority if you wish to make offers that your counterparts can't refuse. The more bargaining power you possess, the more generous you should be with *process*—not *substance*. If you let your counterparts participate in the interaction and feel they influenced the outcome, they will pay you for the privilege by accepting terms that favor your side. We all like to think we had the chance to state our own positions and be heard. To the extent we are granted this privilege, we become more amenable to compromise. On the other hand, when we are presented with *faits accomplis* and are denied the opportunity to alter opponent perceptions, we become frustrated and often refuse to accept opponent terms that may be objectively reasonable.

Managers have to be especially aware of the negative impact of best-offer-first bargaining when they interact with their subordinates. It is difficult for supervisors to interact with subordinates on an "adult"-to-"adult" basis.

They act as "parents" and try to impose on their "child"-like subordinates what they think is good for them. Even when such supervisory offers are rational, the subordinates have a natural tendency to respond in a "child"-like fashion. To demonstrate that they possess options, they must reject the "parental" offer no matter how realistic it may actually be. The "parental" supervisors then react with anger, and the interactions deteriorate.

Whenever you are contemplating best-offer-first bargaining, remember how offensive *you* would find such tactics if your counterparts employed them. Give the other side the opportunity to participate as much as possible in the interaction. Make them transaction partners. It is possible that your counterparts will generate options you never contemplated. Give them the chance to suggest such mutually beneficial alternatives.

If you encounter best-offer-first situations, try not to immediately reject the overtures of your counterparts merely because of the offensive way in which they have announced their initial positions. These are not always devious bargaining counterparts who are trying to hoodwink you. They may be people who are not comfortable with the give-and-take of the bargaining process and who really try to start with reasonable opening offers. Companies like Saturn and Mercedes, which refuse to engage in auction bargaining over the price of cars, are perfect examples. Try to separate the take-it-or-leave-it opening offer from the actual terms being proposed. When you know in your mind that the offer you have just received is what you were hoping to get, accept those terms. Don't cut off your nose to spite your face, as many children are prone to do when given take-it-or-leave-it offers.

FLINCHING OR LOOKING DEJECTED

If your counterpart makes an opening offer (or subsequent concession) you don't like, you can use the following nonverbal signals to generate unreciprocated position changes. Flinch visibly or exhibit a look of complete dejection, and then remain perfectly silent. The technique is designed to induce uncertain counterparts to think their initial offer is wholly unacceptable. In some instances, you may generate two or three unreciprocated position changes, as your counterparts bid against themselves in an effort to placate you.

When counterparts use this device against you, don't make the mistake of providing them with additional offers. Ignore their negative facial expressions. Patiently await their response to your position statement. Don't panic if one or two minutes of silence result. Once your adversaries realize that you won't bid against yourself, they will enter the discussions and state an opening offer (or another concession) of their own.

WRITTEN DOCUMENTS

Many proficient negotiators recognize the aura of legitimacy associated with written documents. They initiate a bargaining encounter by providing the other side with a highly principled opening offer in written form. Since we have been raised to believe that what is written is generally true, we accord their initial position more respect than it deserves. When counterparts provide you with a written memo containing their opening offer, don't accord it more respect than it objectively warrants. Remember that individuals can puff and embellish as quickly on their word processors as they can orally. Examine the proposed terms carefully and decide which items to challenge.

Negotiators can also use written documents to obtain a tactical advantage near the end of bargaining encounters. When you begin to finalize the terms you think have been agreed upon through regular discussions, they present you with written statements—often on pre-printed forms—containing those terms. This approach is often used by landlords through lease forms, and car dealers and real estate agents who use written sales contracts. While they accurately include the terms that have been agreed upon, they usually add language that detracts from what you think you have obtained. For example, the landlord may include language requiring you to clean the carpets and paint the walls when you vacate the premises. Car dealers may include such extras as "transportation costs," "dealer prep," and "processing fees" that increase what you have to pay by $500 to $1,000. Why weren't these items included in the asking price and subsumed within the final figure agreed upon? By leaving these items until the end—after everything else has been agreed to—the landlords and car dealers realize their ability to demand extra concessions once you have become psychologically committed to the transaction.

You may hardly recognize the significance of these extra provisions, and when you do, it is so easy to assume your obligation to accept these items since they are set forth in printed documents. These are all negotiable terms. Don't hesitate to indicate your dissatisfaction with these types of clauses and ask to have them removed or demand concessions in exchange for your acceptance of these terms. Landlords may cross off clean-up provisions if you object to them and they think you will be a good tenant. Car dealers may waive "dealer prep" and "processing fee" items if it is near the end of the model year and they are trying to sell you last year's model, or it is near the end of the month and they hope to receive incentive payments from the manufacturer.

What should you do when you attempt to have preprinted form clauses removed and are told you must accept those terms or go elsewhere? Don't reject good apartments or good car purchases simply because of such add-on clauses. Try to discover during your preparation the degree to which the industry you will be dealing with uses such provisions. This way you will be prepared for them. Ask at the beginning of your interaction about "extra" costs not included in your present discussions. When these items are raised at the conclusion of interactions, politely ask to negotiate over these terms. When your overtures in this regard are rejected, objectively review the final terms and ask whether you are getting a good price, even with these add-ons. If you are, don't scuttle the deal because of them.

LIMITED AUTHORITY

How often have you negotiated with salespersons or immediate supervisors and achieved what you thought were "final" terms only to have the salespeople or supervisors indicate a need to have the final provisions reviewed by the "sales manager" or "division director"? This is an especially common bargaining technique among car dealers. Just as you are about to sign the purchase agreement in front of you, the salesperson steps into the back room—ostensibly to get the approval of the sales manager. When the salesperson reappears, he or she looks distraught. The "sales manager" has rejected the unusually generous terms they have given you, pointing out how far your price is below the "invoice" figure. Dealers who use this device are convinced that most customers are unwilling at this point to walk out and go to other dealerships. The prospective buyers are mentally committed to this transaction, and are not going to allow a few hundred dollars to negate their purchase. If this ploy is used effectively, you even feel sorry for the salesperson and agree to increase what you are paying the dealer to prevent that person from suffering further humiliation. For all you know, you may be presently talking with the sales manager. He or she may have merely gone into the back room to grab a cup of coffee before returning to the sales floor to fleece you!

When you begin to negotiate with salespeople, don't hesitate to ask whether they have final authority. If they indicate that they do not, you may ask to talk directly with the sales manager. Sometimes the sales manager will actually join the conversation. On other occasions, salespeople will indicate that their recommendations are almost always accepted. This puts their reputations on the line and makes it difficult for them to demand concessions at the end without looking foolish. When the dealer demands several concessions at the end as a prerequisite to a final deal, don't hesitate to ask what they can give you in return. Could they include the better CD player or the mag wheels? Could they include the extended warranty for the extra costs you are paying? If you demand reciprocity, you will either obtain some concessions in exchange for what they are demanding or they may give up on their efforts to obtain unilateral changes from you. If you are unable to get them to withdraw their new demands, you can either head for the exit—hoping they will call you back before you get out the door—or accept those new terms as part of the deal.

Never make the mistake of negotiating with individuals who have absolutely no bargaining authority. This occasionally happens when people from the other side contact you—usually by telephone—to find out what you hope to obtain. When you explain your opening offer, they indicate how unacceptable your stated terms are, suggesting that they could not even convey that position to their superiors. They hope that you will become embarrassed and make another offer. If they can induce you to bid against yourself through consecutive opening offers, they will gain a substantial bargaining advantage. Never make consecutive opening offers in response to these people. When they initially criticize your opening terms, *ask them* what *they* are willing to offer you. If they indicate they have no bargaining authority, tell them to get some authority and place their own offer on the table so you can discuss the merits of your respective positions.

NIBBLING

Some manipulative negotiators seemingly agree to final accords. Their counterparts are pleased with the agreements and consider the deals finished. Several days later, these negotiators contact their counterparts with apparent embarrassment and indicate they must have several "small" changes in the terms agreed upon. Often combined with the "limited authority" ploy, nibblers use their absent superiors as the basis for the last-minute changes being demanded. House buyers often use this approach after entering into binding sales contracts. As the closing dates approach, they find minor problems with the properties they are purchasing and request price reductions to reflect these unanticipated conditions.

I once met a successful business attorney who told me that at the conclusion of every major negotiation he demands several last-minute changes. He claimed that his demands have always been met by his counterparts. I told him he was a *nibbler* and explained the concept as follows. The attorney agreed that he fit the definition and said that this technique is always successful.

If you are confronted by demands for small changes made by nibbling counterparts, you are in trouble. By this point in the negotiations, you are psychologically committed to a final agreement, and most often do not want these last-minute demands to negate your previous efforts. You are likely to give in to the modest changes being requested. If you find yourself being nibbled, don't make the mistake of asking the wrong question: "Am *I* going to allow the whole deal to fall through over these few items?" Instead, focus on your *counterparts*. Ask yourself whether you think your *counterparts* will let the entire deal collapse over these few terms. Use that answer to guide you.

When counterparts employ the nibble technique to obtain last-minute concessions from you, *demand reciprocity*. When they contact you and describe the "slight" changes they require, indicate how relieved you are that they have called and suggest how dissatisfied you are with respect to several terms—and request changes in those provisions. If your counterparts are truly sincere and are not trying to fleece you, they will recognize the need for reciprocity when they request last-minute concessions. They will offer to give you some of what you want in exchange for the modifications they are seeking. If they are nibblers, however, they will reject further discussions and demand that you honor the *original terms* agreed upon.

Always remember to demand reciprocal concessions from your nibbling adversaries. Nibblers are pick-pockets. They hope to steal several items from you at the conclusion of bargaining interactions. It is important to remember that when they put their hand in your pocket to extract something from you, you should put your hand in their pocket to obtain reciprocal concessions.

Range Offers

Some negotiators phrase their monetary offers in terms of a range, rather than as a single figure. For example, realtors may indicate that their sellers hope to obtain a price in the "$250,000 to $265,000 area." Prospective buyers may similarly state their willingness to pay something in the "$240,000 to $255,000 range." Some negotiators who wish to establish more conciliatory bargaining environments may use this technique to evidence their receptivity to compromise. However, this approach, more often than not, indicates uncertainty in the minds of those making the offers. More carefully prepared and more confident bargainers determine the exact amount they are willing to pay or accept and announce that figure at this point.

In most cases, it is advisable to avoid range offers when the serious discussions begin. On the other hand, if you are asked during preliminary talks regarding a new employment opportunity about the salary you would have to have, it may be appropriate for you to mention a range to prevent an excessive demand from eliminating you from consideration. Once you have received the offer, and you are negotiating the actual compensation you will receive, it is preferable to mention the true amount you expect to get. After you have received the offer, the balance of power shifts in your favor, because the offering firm wants to obtain the services of the individual it has decided to hire.

When you receive range offers, focus on the end of the range that favors your situation. For example, if you were looking for a new house, and the prospective seller indicated that she would have to have something in the $250,000 to $265,000 range, respond as if you have been given a $250,000 demand. Similarly, if you are selling your home and a prospective purchaser says he is willing to pay something in the $240,000 to $255,000 range, treat that statement as a $255,000 offer. If you do this adroitly, the offerors will accept your characterization of their offers and continue the discussion as if they had mentioned the specific figures being cited by you.

Decreasing or Limited Duration Offers

On some occasions, you may want to make an offer on something but wish to obtain a quick response from the person to whom you are making the offer. For example, you are a book publisher. You may be willing to make an offer on a book proposal that a literary agent has submitted for consideration, but only want to give the agent a day or so to respond. If they don't accept your offer, you plan to withdraw your offer. Don't hesitate to place a specific limitation in your offer indicating that it is good for one day or forty-eight hours and is thereafter withdrawn. This limits the ability of the seller to use your offer to whipsaw other publishers who have also expressed interest in the book proposal into new offers of their own. It also lets the agent know that if she does not act quickly, either to accept your offer or to make a realistic counteroffer, she will lose you as a prospective purchaser.

On rare occasions you may make an offer with the stipulation that the terms are only good for one week; after that, you will reduce your offer by a specified amount to take into account circumstances you believe will change over that time period. If you decide to use this technique, be absolutely clear about the entire scope of your offer. If you fail to do so and reduce (or withdraw) your offer a week later, claims of bad faith negotiating are likely to arise. It is generally assumed when negotiators make offers that they will remain on the table for a reasonable period of time without being reduced or withdrawn. We thus have an obligation to tell counterparts of our intention to alter this assumption. One last factor should also be recognized. Never tell someone you plan to reduce or withdraw your offer at a certain time unless you are fully prepared to honor that commitment. To do so would be a threat, and if you fail to carry out your threat when the other side calls your bluff, your credibility will be lost.

ANGER

Raising cain during the critical stage of a negotiation can be an effective way to convince recalcitrant counterparts of the seriousness of your position. Raised voices and table pounding may intimidate adversaries and convince them to give you what you are seeking. Keep in mind that when proficient negotiators exhibit anger, it is usually carefully controlled behavior. Intelligent Negotiators never lose their tempers. They realize that if they did, they would be likely to say or do something that would injure their bargaining interests.

I have seen labor negotiators resort to anger during important points in bargaining discussions. They stand up, raise their voices, swear at their counterparts, pound the bargaining table, and then storm out of the room. They appear to be outraged by what they are complaining about. Yet, once they enter their side's separate caucus room, they calmly say: "How did I do? I thought I was quite believable!" Their outburst was completely orchestrated to intimidate their counterparts into further movement, and it often worked.

If your counterparts get angry, do not respond in kind. If they yell, swear, head for the door, or slam down the telephone, do not try to beat them to it. Step back and realize that most anger exhibited during bargaining encounters is controlled behavior. Instead of responding in kind, it is preferable that you become quiet and remain professional. Listen carefully to what your shouting counterparts are saying. No matter how carefully they try to control their apparent diatribes, there will be verbal leaks. They can't choose every word perfectly, and often give away important information. You should also look for nonverbal signals. As they continue their harangue, your quiet presence will begin to embarrass them. It is difficult to yell at someone who is looking at you as if you are behaving like a child. Once your counterparts calm down and take their seats, you should point out your recent concessions and ask them how they could cast aspersions on someone who has been as reasonable as you have been. You hope to generate guilt to go along with the embarrassment they are experiencing. If you are successful, the party doing all the shouting will be induced to make the next concession!

AGGRESSIVE BEHAVIOR

Negotiators who employ aggressive tactics hope to intimidate weaker counterparts and induce them to cave in to their demands. They attempt to dominate the initial discussions the moment they enter the room. They loudly state their position and tell you that you must accede to their terms. They attempt to seize control over the bargaining agenda in an effort to dictate the items to be discussed. When you encounter such people, it is important to remember that they cannot force you to say "yes" to their demands. Sooner or later, even the most aggressive bargainers have to become quiet and allow you to state your position. While they are speaking, listen carefully for verbal leaks and watch for nonverbal signals. Patiently wait for them to wear themselves out. Once they are silent, you can make your points. If they try to disrupt your presentation through rude interruptions, calmly inform them that you are not finished. If they continue to interrupt, you can more forcefully indicate that you don't talk when they are speaking and don't expect them to talk while you are speaking. Through such "attitudinal bargaining," you can set some ground rules for how you are going to proceed.

A few aggressive negotiators also employ a highly adversarial style. They may even use sarcasm to insult counterparts. Try to get them to modify their offensive behavior by telling them you are unwilling to participate in discussions that are not carried out in a professional manner. If you don't believe you can alter the nasty conduct of such people but must deal with them over some important points, use the telephone as much as possible. You don't see them when they are insulting you, and they are unable to bask in your dejected demeanor. When you begin to feel uneasy, indicate that you have another phone call and politely hang up, promising to call them back when you are free. This allows you to control the interactions in a way that diminishes their ability to bother you.

It is particularly important when you're dealing with offensive adversaries to try to separate the people from the problems that have to be negotiated. You can set a good example for unpleasant counterparts by being especially courteous yourself. Patiently listen to their side, and try to place yourself in their shoes. If you can demonstrate your appreciation for their position, they may become less confrontational. If they have stated the issues to be resolved in a one-sided fashion, it can be helpful to reframe the issues using less emotional language. If the parties can agree on neutral position statements, they will enhance their ability to achieve mutual accords.

Some aggressive negotiators are simply bullies. They don't even pretend to negotiate; they demand no less than complete capitulation. Never permit counterparts to do this to you. When you encounter highly threatening counterparts, carefully review your non-settlement alternatives and ask whether what they are offering is preferable to what you could achieve through other avenues. Remember that underneath most bullies lies a coward. They huff and puff, but rarely carry out their dire threats. When people bully you, indicate your willingness to accept your non-settlement alternatives. Try to exude an inner peace that indicates that you are comfortable with that choice if it becomes necessary. Soon after you accept the possibility of a non-settlement, the dynamic between you and your bullying counterparts begins to change. As those people realize that the negotiations may fail, they examine their own non-settlement options and realize that they are better off dealing with you. They begin to fear the consequences associated with stalled talks, and begin to exhibit a more conciliatory manner.

WALKING OUT/SLAMMING DOWN THE TELEPHONE

Some demonstrative negotiators occasionally resort to extreme tactics to convince counterparts that they are unwilling to make additional concessions. As the parties approach final terms, they storm out of the room or slam down the telephone. This induces risk-adverse counterparts to close all or most of the gap remaining between the parties. While this tactic can be quite effective when you use it against overly anxious counterparts who fear the consequences associated with non-settlements, you run the very real risk of causing a complete breakdown in the bargaining process.

When counterparts resort to these techniques, *never* make the mistake of running after them or immediately phoning back the individuals who have deliberately short-circuited your telephone discussions. Your counterparts would view such behavior on your part as a sign of great weakness. If your negotiating counterparts resort to extreme tactics, be patient. Give them time to cool down and to appreciate the fact that you have not been intimidated by this device. When the time is right, the parties will regenerate the stalled negotiations in recognition of the fact that mutual accords are almost always preferable to stalemates.

If you are negotiating in your counterpart's office and she storms out, remain where you are. After departing, she will probably become paranoid, fearing that you may look at her notes or files. Within five to ten minutes, she will return to her office feeling ashamed of her behavior. She will be so embarrassed that she may even make the next concession.

MUTT AND JEFF (GOOD COP/BAD COP)

The Mutt and Jeff "good cop/bad cop" routine is one of the most common and most effective bargaining ploys. It works as follows: You, a seemingly reasonable negotiator (Good Cop) soften counterpart resistance by acknowledging the generous position changes that the counterparts have made. You then lead them to believe that a final accord is on the horizon if only they could make several additional concessions. When they take the bait and make the requested position changes, their optimism is crushed by your teammate (Bad Cop) who attacks the propriety of their new offer. Bad Cop castigates the counterparts for their meager concessions and insincere desire to achieve a final accord. Just as your counterparts are preparing to explode at Bad Cop, you assuage their feelings by suggesting that if several additional concessions are made, you could probably induce Bad Cop to accept the new terms. Generally, counterparts will succumb to this and make the requested position changes, only to encounter further attacks from the unreasonable participant. It is amazing how diligently negotiators work to formulate terms that will satisfy Bad Cop.

Devious negotiators may employ the Mutt and Jeff technique with the controlling participant assuming the role of the "reasonable" negotiator. To do this, instruct your partner to reject every new offer in an enraged and belittling manner. Bad Cop may even be allowed to head for the exit on occasion—until you prevail upon him or her to return to the discussions. Careless negotiators may become so afraid of the "unreasonable" person's wrath, they work to placate their demands and conclude the interaction.

The Mutt and Jeff approach may even be used when you need to bolster your bargaining strength. You can do this as a single negotiator by portraying your absent "superior" as the "unreasonable" party whose extreme demands must be satisfied. Car salespeople often use the absent "sales manager" as the ogre who must be placated. They praise potential buyers for their generous concessions and sincere efforts to achieve mutually acceptable terms, but insist on additional position changes to satisfy their absent partner. Immediate supervisors who are being asked for pay raises may use their absent superiors as "unreasonable" tightwads who are demanding that wage increases be kept within specified limits. Negotiators often utilize this device to great effect because it allows them to maintain a congenial relationship with their counterparts by sympathetically telling them you think their terms are reasonable. If only you did not have to gain the approval of your "unreasonable" boss, you would be able to give them the generous deal you think they deserve.

When you encounter what appear to be Mutt and Jeff counterparts, don't confront them about it. If they are deliberately employing this tactic, they will never admit it. If they are not using it deliberately, and one opponent actually disagrees with his or her partner's unrealistic assessment, accusing them of disingenuous negotiating would offend and create a tense bargaining atmosphere.

Don't make the mistake, however, of allowing the seemingly unreasonable participant to control the bargaining. You can do this by including the *reasonable* Good Cop in the discussions, rather than direct your arguments and offers exclusively to the Bad Cop. When the Good Cop requests position changes that are designed to satisfy the demands of his unreasonable partner, directly ask him if *he* would be willing to accept your terms if you made those changes. On rare occasions, the seemingly reasonable participant may actually indicate a willingness to accept your new offer, despite the protestations of his unreasonable partner. Such circumstances would indicate that your counterparts are not really using the Good Cop/Bad Cop approach but are having a strong disagreement about their side's true needs. Once you induce one opponent to accept your new terms, it is much harder for his partner to continue to hold out. Try to whipsaw the reasonable person against his unrealistic partner.

If your counterparts are really employing the Good Cop/Bad Cop technique, the "reasonable" participant will never agree with your proposed terms. He will instead suggest that if those changes were formally offered, he would seek the approval of his "unreasonable" partner. When this happens, ask them one more time whether they would be willing to accept the deal if you were to make the position changes they are requesting. Force them to say "yes" or "no." They will most likely continue to blame their inability to agree to your terms on their "unreasonable" partners—and they will look foolish doing so.

Irrationality or Crazy Like a Fox

I am frequently asked how to deal with wholly irrational negotiators. From the number of stories I hear about lawyers and business leaders, I get the impression that most of them are in need of institutionalization! Very few of the individuals who exhibit bizarre behavior during bargaining encounters are insane; they are "crazy like a fox." People who use this tactic hope to convince counterparts that they cannot be dealt with logically. Counterparts must either give in to their one-sided demands or face the consequences associated with ongoing negotiations with unstable parties. Do not allow seemingly unstable personalities to blind you to your own non-settlement options, for that is the name of this game.

A federal judge I know once told me that whenever he is assigned a complex case he would prefer not to try, he waits until a couple of weeks before the scheduled trial date. He invites the attorneys into his chambers and asks them to summarize the legal issues involved. They always do an excellent job. When they are done, he asks them several questions that are completely off the wall. They look at each other and panic. They can't let this irrational judge preside over their case. They rush outside and settle their dispute. The judge gets to play golf on Wednesday afternoons with the doctors and dentists!

The most effective way to counter such feigned irrationality is to ignore it and respond in an entirely rational manner. Once your counterparts realize that their seemingly irrational behavior is not having the planned impact, they will reconsider their approach. Furthermore, when the negotiators take a break to evaluate their respective circumstances, these individuals will analyze your offers as logically as other counterparts.

Some business negotiators use a combination of limited authority, Mutt and Jeff, and irrationality to advance their interests. They describe their supervisors as mean and irrational ogres who must be placated if final deals are to be achieved. They hope to intimidate you into unwarranted concessions. Car salespeople may paint sales managers in this light, and some human resource workers may describe their superiors in this way, hoping that you will not question their refusal to make more generous job offers. When you encounter these negotiators, don't hesitate to request your own direct discussions with the sales manager or the head of human resources. Your request is likely to be denied, but the individuals you are dealing with should become more accommodating as a result of your entreaty.

On rare occasions, you may encounter truly irrational counterparts. They usually present you with non-negotiable demands and refuse to listen to reasoned arguments to the contrary. Appreciate the fact that it is impossible to reason with such people. If you could, they would not be irrational. You have to carefully review your own non-settlement alternatives and determine whether they are preferable to what your crazy counterparts are demanding. If your external options are preferable, accept them.

FALSE DEMANDS

Alert negotiators often discover during the Information Exchange that their counterparts want to obtain items that they themselves do not value. Once you discover this situation, you can exploit this fact by emphasizing your own side's interest in these terms. Put this technique to use trading substantial position changes for what to you are insignificant concessions. Remember the value of bargaining items is always defined by those persons who want them. If I have something you desire, you will give me something of value to get it.

You can include false demands in negotiation packages. That may induce counterparts to give you what you really hope to achieve. Suppose you have to negotiate with your supervisor over three things you really want. If you are wondering whether or not to bring just the three items into negotiations, don't. If you only ask for these three terms, your superior may reject at least one to remind you who has the bargaining power. Is there something else you could request that would be wholly unacceptable to your supervisor? Include this item in your initial request. When your superior questions your right to the other three items, offer to trade one of those terms for this particular provision. You will probably get all three of the terms you desire—with your superior being relieved that you were willing to yield on the one item he or she found unpalatable!

The use of false items has one serious risk associated with it. If you demand terms your counterparts really don't wish to have, they may use your own disingenuous demands to obtain concessions on items you really value. Before you ever insist on issues you think your counterparts want, be certain during the information exchange that you are right. What if you make a mistake in this regard and get stuck with something you don't want? Near the conclusion of the closing stage, slowly move into the cooperative mode and offer to trade that item for another term you prefer. Don't admit your disingenuous bargaining tactics. This may undermine the whole deal.

Alleged Expertise

Some negotiators attempt to overwhelm counterparts with technical details that are designed to intimidate less knowledgeable individuals. Car mechanics have used this technique for decades, and computer technicians now employ this approach. They explain the area that must be negotiated in such technical terms that it is impossible for laypeople to understand the real problem. They want customers to think they have no choice, that their machine may never function again. Once such negotiators accomplish this, they can usually bank on customer approval for expensive repairs. The customers may even think they are getting a real bargain given the complicated problems involved.

When you encounter counterparts who try to overwhelm you with technical jargon, praise them for their knowledge but politely ask them to explain the situation in lay terms. If they still use incomprehensible language, ask questions that will force them to indicate what is actually wrong. Never accept the premise that they are so intelligent that they can't explain things to someone as unsophisticated as you. If they are really that bright, they should be able to describe their field in a way others can comprehend. Tell them that you can't authorize the expensive work they are requesting if you are unable to understand the problem to be fixed.

Weakening a More Powerful Counterpart

How do you deal with counterparts who possess more bargaining power than you do? People often ask me this in my seminars. I try to point out what young children recognize intuitively: There is no such thing as bargaining power, but only the perception of it. If I *think* you possess power and you know how to use my belief in your power to your advantage, then you have bargaining power. If, however, I don't believe you possess any real authority, you will begin to question your own power. Parents think they have authority when they negotiate with their children. Children learn to ignore parental power, and it disappears almost instantly. It is the ability of children to ignore parental power that both drives parents crazy and enables the children to win most parent-child interactions.

Of course, no two negotiators have equal amounts of time, resources, options, and so on, but your willingness to walk away if necessary equalizes bargaining strength. You are at the table together because each of you wants something from the other. When you negotiate with others who appear to possess greater authority than you have, try to ignore their superior power. Calmly negotiate as if you are perfectly willing to accept your non-settlement options if that course becomes necessary. The more you are able to exude an inner confidence in your own situation, the more your counterparts will begin to question their own bargaining authority. Before you know it, they will accord you more respect than you may objectively deserve.

ENHANCING YOUR OWN BARGAINING STRENGTH

How can you improve your circumstances when you find yourself with minimal bargaining authority? If you are negotiating on behalf of a large organization, use a combination of *Limited Authority* and *Mutt and Jeff* to enhance your bargaining authority. Directly acknowledge the reasonableness of the terms being proposed by the other side, but indicate that your absent superior thinks you should obtain better terms. Tell your counterparts that if they fail to propose more generous terms, your superior will refuse to accept the deal. Before you know it, your adversaries will strive to satisfy the needs of your absent partner. The fact that your superior may be perfectly satisfied with what is currently being offered is irrelevant, as long as you are able to convince your counterparts that better terms are needed to generate the acceptance of your absent partner.

In some instances, you may be able to publicly lock yourself into positions that would be difficult to alter without suffering a substantial loss of face. This is quite effective. Announce to your counterparts in front of your superior that if you are unable to obtain certain terms, you will fail your firm. If you are negotiating to purchase a new car with your spouse, you could indicate in front of that person that you would be incompetent if you paid more than a specified amount for the vehicle you are considering. This would force your counterparts to choose between trying to get you to capitulate, which they know would greatly embarrass you in front of your superior or your spouse, and giving you a better deal.

BARGAINING WITH INFLEXIBLE COUNTERPARTS

It is extremely frustrating to negotiate with counterparts who are unalterably committed to positions that are unacceptable to you. While you may be tempted to directly challenge their uncompromising stands, this may anger them and cause them to become even more unyielding. It is more productive to employ a less confrontational approach that provides your adversaries with a face-saving means of altering their obstinate dispositions. Try to induce such inflexible adversaries to step back from their stated positions and revisit the objective criteria underlying their positions. Keep in mind that it is much easier to generate position reappraisals through a needs and interests analysis than through discussions that focus directly on the stated positions.

Another effective strategy for dealing with intransigent counterparts is to emphasize the areas of agreement, rather than the areas of conflict. Bring the discussion back to the areas in which joint gain is possible. Both sides will reaffirm your commitment to final agreements, and the areas of conflict will seem less critical.

USING FALSE CONCESSIONS

False concessions are effective when they generate guilt in the other party. Negotiators can accomplish this in two ways:

1. You can make concessions on items that you have no right to demand in the first place. A good example of this is the car dealer who agrees to drop the "dealer prep" or "processing fee" if the buyer agrees to raise his or her offer. These are dealer add-ons that simply increase their profit margin. Since such items do not really add to their cost, customers should not be expected to pay extra for these terms after they have agreed upon the spe-

cific price to be paid for the vehicle. Negotiators should always be wary of items cited by counterparts that do not increase the true value of what the participants are exchanging.

2. Make multiple position changes that make your counterpart think you have moved more than you had originally planned to move. This is exemplified by the car salesperson who asks for $24,000, moves to $23,750, to $23,500, and finally to $23,300 without any counteroffers from the prospective buyer. This individual then suggests that he or she has conceded more than he or she should have and says that further movement is impossible. The salesperson hopes to make the buyer feel guilty about this "excessive" movement and induce him or her to make a larger counteroffer. Whenever counterparts do this to you, remember that the critical factor is not *how many* concessions they have made, but *how far* they have actually moved. Base your decision on the actual distance they have closed between you.

PREDICTING DISASTER

Negotiators can obtain a bargaining advantage at critical points by threatening dire consequences if agreements are not achieved quickly. This tactic goes beyond *threats*. Here you talk as if the world will end should your counterparts not give in to your demands. Careless or naive bargainers may be influenced by this ploy, especially when they focus entirely on the harm *they* will suffer if the threatened consequences occurred. When teachers' unions first obtained collective bargaining rights, school districts used this technique against them. As negotiations progressed, the school district would announce the need to lay off all the untenured teachers if the union did not reduce its wage demands. The threatened teachers often panicked and reduced their requested pay increases. If they had evaluated the situation objectively, they would have seen through this idle threat. If all untenured teachers were actually laid off, the English or History departments would be understaffed and the school district would no longer be eligible for state educational funding. Over the years, teachers' unions have become more sophisticated, and school districts resort to this tactic less often than they once did.

When your counterparts threaten extreme consequences if you do not yield to their positions, ask yourself two questions:

1. Are the threatened consequences likely to occur? When you step back and evaluate the situation objectively, you may realize that your counterpart could not possibly do what they are threatening.

2. If the negative results might occur, how would those results affect your *counterparts*? In many cases, if the threatened consequences were to occur, they would be more devastating for your adversaries than for yourself. When this is true, your counterparts would be crazy to take a course of action that would hurt them far more than you.

PLAYING BRER RABBIT

In his classic book *Uncle Remus*,[1] Joel Chandler Harris created the unforgettable Brer Rabbit. When Brer Rabbit is caught by the fox, he tells the fox he can drown him, roast him, or skin him, so long as he does not throw him in the briar-patch. Since the fox is intent on punishing Brer Rabbit, he chooses the one alternative the rabbit seems to fear most; he throws Brer Rabbit in the briar-patch, and Brer Rabbit is able to escape unharmed.

Brer Rabbit is a "reverse psychology" ploy that can be especially effective against adversarial *win-lose* counter-parts who judge their success more by how poorly you do than by how well they do. When you encounter such bar-gaining partners, initially demand your secondary objec-tives—items A, B, C, D, and E. Then indicate that at a minimum you would have to have X, Y, and Z, which are your real first choices. If you are convincing, your win-lose counterparts will literally force on you items X, Y, and Z! You have to play the game to the end, which means sug-gesting that these are your least beneficial items and by asking if they could possibly give you some other terms. Your counterparts will smile as they reject your request for better terms, believing they have annihilated you!

I had a dean at another law school who always gave faculty members their second choices to demonstrate who held the bargaining power. One of my colleagues was thinking of submitting a request for a monetary grant he desired. He could either obtain this financial support by teaching summer school or by agreeing to work on a re-search project. In prior years, he had indicated his prefer-ence for a research stipend, but had always been given his second choice—a summer teaching assignment. When he told me about these experiences, I suggested that he describe a summer teaching assignment as his first choice, with the research stipend being his second choice. Since summer teaching duties paid more, this did not seem disingenuous. He was afraid the dean would give him his insincere "first choice." I replied that the dean never gave anyone their stated preference. With great reluctance, he listed summer teaching as his first choice, with a research stipend as his fallback alternative. Several days later, the dean notified him that it was not possible to give him the summer teaching assignment he had requested, forcing him to accept the research stipend he actually wished to obtain.

Never use Brer Rabbit against normal win-win opponents. If you demand items A, B, C, D, and E from win-win counterparts, they may think you are being sincere and give you the items you don't really wish to obtain. Only use the Brer Rabbit approach against extreme win-lose adversaries who hope to destroy you by forcing on you the terms they think you least hope to get.

ASKING "SO WHAT?"

When negotiators make concessions, they want to be sure their counterparts give them credit for their position changes. You can sometimes obtain a bargaining advantage by suggesting that your counterpart's concessions are worthless to you. They may improve their offer or make additional concessions in response. However, never permit your counterparts to do this to you. If they try to devalue your new offers, indicate how valuable what you have given up is to you and ask whether they would mind if you kept those items for yourself. If they are really of no value to your counterparts, they should not mind if you withdrew them. You will be amazed how quickly your counterparts will protest when you try to reclaim the items they disingenuously indicated were of minimal value to themselves!

APPEARING DISINTERESTED

Along similar lines, you can sometimes instill doubt and get your counterpart to make a position change by appearing disinterested when he or she is making important points. But never permit counterparts to do this to you. If they try to ignore your presentation, ask them probing questions, such as "What are the weaknesses you perceive in my position?" Ask them to state the terms they need to obtain. Ask them to explain the reasons for the positions they are taking. Through such questions, you can force seemingly disinterested parties to become more participative.

GOING BELLY-UP

Belly-Up is one bargaining technique that is especially difficult to counter. It entails acting like a wolf in sheepskin. A Belly-Up negotiator wears old clothes and likes to negotiate at the homes or offices of his or her counterparts. When using this approach, indicate how lovely the environment of your counterpart is when you arrive. Then profess your own lack of negotiating ability and praise your counterpart for his or her reputation as a highly skilled negotiator. You can use this self-deprecating approach to evoke your counterpart's sympathy and lure him or her into a false sense of security.

The epitome of the Belly-Up approach was artfully created by actor Peter Falk in his Lt. Columbo police detective character. The inspector seemed to bumble along during criminal investigations with no apparent plan. When he interviewed suspects, he did so in a completely disorganized manner. By the time suspects realized that Lt. Columbo really understood what was going on, they had confessed and were in police custody!

Belly-Up negotiators are among the most difficult people to deal with because they do not participate normally in the bargaining process. Using feigned incompetence allows you to forego engaging in the usual give-and-take. So does professing your total inability to know what would be a fair result and asking your counterpart—the recognized expert—to suggest terms he thinks would be equitable.

Although your counterpart had planned a tough opening position and established a high aspiration level, his conscience begins to bother him. He can't take complete advantage of you, the incompetent opponent, so he significantly modifies his planned opening position in your direction. Now you've got him. Praise him immediately for his generosity and obvious effort to do what is right, and then indicate why his proposed terms would not be sufficient to satisfy your particular needs. "*Yes* you have made a generous offer, *but* those items would not be sufficient with respect to X and Y." He quickly suggests changes in the hopes of satisfying your newly stated needs, only to have you once again indicate the need for further movement. By the time he is able to obtain your assent to his proposals, he is naked! You have adroitly stripped him of everything. The most amazing thing is that your counterpart feels so good about his ability to satisfy the needs of his pathetic counterpart that he can hardly wait to assist you in future encounters.

You should never allow seemingly inept counterparts evoke such sympathy that they induce you to concede everything. It is not fair for one side to make the other party do all the work. Don't permit practitioners of this technique to get you to alter your planned approach. If you are bargaining with a Belly-Up negotiator, articulate your originally formulated position at the outset. When she appears totally disappointed and requests immediate modifications, ask *her* to state and defend *her own opening position*. It is the last thing she is prepared to do. She hopes to get you to state your position and continually alter it until it suits her needs. By compelling her to articulate her own position, you will force her to participate. You can then challenge the terms of her proposal and force her to defend the items she has requested. Belly-Up negotiators are not used to discussing their own positions. Once you place them in this position, their ability to make you do all the work is negated and they are forced to resume normal bargaining.

I have met several lawyers who told me that when negotiations become difficult, they place their hand over their heart and have a pained expression on their face. If this doesn't moderate opponent behavior, they reach into their desk drawer and take out a vial of what appears to be nitroglycerin tablets. A rather perceptive and assertive female attorney I know once encountered such an opponent. When he placed his hand over his heart, she continued her tough negotiating tactics. When he withdrew the "nitroglycerin" vial, she didn't alter her behavior. He couldn't understand why his Belly-Up approach was not affecting her conduct—until she finally asked him what his time was in the marathon the prior weekend. Both negotiators had run in the same race, and he had worn such a colorful outfit that she remembered him. She thus knew he had no heart problem. The closest that attorney ever came to a heart attack was when she asked him about his time in the marathon. He became so disconcerted that he had to leave his office to regain his composure. After he returned, he gave up the Belly-Up charade.

In some instances, particular negotiation ploys may be used in isolation (such as the "Belly-Up" ploy). In most instances, however, two or more different techniques are brought to bear simultaneously or in sequence in an effort to keep adversaries off balance (for example, "Mutt and Jeff," "Anger," and "Limited Authority"). When you negotiate, carefully monitor the tactics being employed by your counterparts. This is the best way to counteract them when they are being used against you.

PASSIVE-AGGRESSIVE NEGOTIATING

A Passive-Aggressive negotiator is as difficult to deal with as a Belly-Up bargainer. Instead of directly challenging their counterpart's tactics and proposals, they employ devices that indirectly disrupt the negotiation process. They usually appear to be laidback and disinterested. They may show up late for scheduled meetings and fail to return their counterpart's phone calls. They may forget to bring important documents to scheduled bargaining sessions. They lead unsuspecting adversaries to think they don't care whether agreements are achieved. If they weren't interested, why would they continue to meet with you? But they are *not* laidback persons. They are in fact extremely aggressive persons who display their anger indirectly.

The negotiators who use Passive-Aggressive techniques are those who dislike the bargaining process. They find the usual give-and-take and the need for concessionary bargaining distasteful. Since Passive-Aggressive negotiators are either unable or unwilling to express their concerns directly, they attempt to disrupt the process indirectly.

When you find yourself across the table from Passive-Aggressive counterparts, neutralize their ability to disrupt the process. First, try to formulate a minimal package you can reasonably defend. Include terms that clearly favor your own interests, but which appear to satisfy the opposing side's basic needs. When you present this proposal to them, they are unlikely to reject the terms outright. They will probably accept your proposed terms, and then demand the opportunity to prepare the agreement incorporating those conditions. When you get together a few days later, ostensibly to finalize the draft they have prepared, they indicate that they were unable to draw up the draft agreement. They suggest further discussions designed to extract additional concessions from you.

During the period they are supposedly preparing the draft agreement, prepare an agreement of your own incorporating the terms that were previously agreed upon. When your counterparts indicate that they were unable to complete this task, open your drawer and pull out your own draft, indicating that you had some extra time that week and decided to do so in case they were too busy. This will enrage them, but they will not or can not express their anger so directly. They will instead review your draft, and are likely to sign it meekly.

SPLITTING THE DIFFERENCE

A popular technique that can be used to achieve final agreements is splitting the distance remaining between the parties' respective positions. This is most appropriately used following detailed bargaining that has brought the parties close together. When you agree to split the difference, you are using the *promise* technique to generate simultaneous movement. You indicate that if your counterparts are willing to go halfway, you are willing to do the same. This can be an especially effective way to close the remaining gap without either side losing face.

Whenever counterparts ask you to split the remaining difference near the conclusion of bargaining interactions, stop and think before you agree. Carefully review in your mind the previous bargaining sequence. Try to determine whether your counterparts skewed the apparent settlement range in their favor through either a biased opening offer or less generous position changes during the distributive and closing stages. Be sure you would not be moving too much in the direction of your counterparts before you agree to meet them "halfway."

NEGOTIATING VIA TELEPHONE

A substantial percentage of business and personal negotiations are conducted wholly or partially on the telephone, since face-to-face meetings may be expensive or inconvenient. Telephone negotiations involve the same stages and bargaining techniques as personal interactions; however, they usually consist of a series of short exchanges rather than longer encounters. Many negotiators who engage in telephone talks make the mistake of treating these electronic exchanges less seriously than they would face-to-face interactions. Since their counterparts can't see them, they think they can wing it on the phone. This is a big mistake.

Do not assume your counterparts cannot read your nonverbal messages on the phone. Many people are better able to hear verbal leaks and discern nonverbal signals during telephone exchanges than during in-person encounters. In a home or office meeting, we are distracted by what's outside the window or how our counterpart has designed the office. On the telephone, however, we are listening intently to the one relevant stimulus—the voice of our counterpart. We are more likely to hear verbal leaks that give away important information, and be more aware of nonverbal signals. We carefully monitor the pitch, pace, tone, and volume of speaker voices. A pregnant pause from a person who did not hesitate before rejecting prior proposals may indicate that this person is seriously considering a particular offer. The pausing party can't disguise the lapse by playing with his glasses or stroking his chin when he is talking on the telephone. A slight sigh in response to a new offer—which is more discernible on the telephone than in person—may similarly indicate interest in your most recent position statement.

Voice inflection can be equally informative. Counterparts who respond to communicated offers with increased levels of excitement suggest that they are more pleased with proposals than their verbal responses indicate. Voice inflection may also suggest speaker deception. As noted earlier, liars tend to speak more deliberately when they misstate information, and the pitch of their voice often goes up.

When you schedule telephone negotiations, prepare as thoroughly for those interactions as you would for in-person talks. You can gain a bargaining advantage by being the one to call your counterpart. If you are lucky, the counterpart won't be prepared for your call, and may begin to think out loud on the phone. If you listen carefully, you may hear verbal leaks and discern a number of nonverbal signals. If, on the other hand, a counterpart catches you off guard with unexpected phone calls when you are not prepared to negotiate, don't hesitate to tell this person that you are busy and will return her call as soon as you are free. Take the time you need to prepare for the encounter, and then call back. When you return the call, don't make the mistake of immediately launching into a discussion of the topics to be exchanged. Since *your counterpart* initiated the exchange, wait until she answers the phone and indicate that you are returning her call. If you then become silent, she will feel the need to speak—and so begin the real talks.

One clear *disadvantage* of telephone negotiations derives from their less personal nature. It is easier for people to say no or to be nasty to someone they can't see. As a result, negotiators are often more inclined to use overtly competitive or adversarial tactics on the phone. When you have to conduct serious bargaining involving critical issues, you may find it beneficial to negotiate face-to-face. The benefits that can be derived from negotiating in person outweigh the increased monetary costs.

NEGOTIATING BY MAIL OR THROUGH FAX OR E-MAIL TRANSMISSIONS

An increasing number of people conduct serious negotiations almost entirely through letters, fax transmissions, or e-mail exchanges. Most people who attempt to restrict their bargaining exchanges to mail, fax, or e-mail are uncomfortable with the split-second decision-making that occurs during personal interactions in the traditional negotiating process. They forget that bargaining involves uniquely *personal interactions* that are not effectively conducted through only written communications.

The use of mail, fax, or e-mail transmissions to conduct basic negotiations is a cumbersome and inefficient process. Each communication must be carefully drafted and thoroughly edited before being sent to the other side. The recipients must read and digest all the written communication, and then formulate their own replies. Written positions seem more intractable than oral statements because of the definitive nature of written documents. When people present proposals orally, their voice inflections and nonverbal signals may indicate a willingness to be flexible with respect to certain items. Written communications rarely convey such information.

Mail, fax, and e-mail exchanges are also more easily misinterpreted. As recipients of such messages read and reread particular passages, they may read more or less into the stated terms than was intended by the senders.

There is nothing wrong with the exchange of written proposals—especially where many complicated terms must be considered. Nonetheless, personal communication should follow major written exchanges. Several days after you have sent a written proposal to a counterpart, telephone that person to *hear* his or her response to your proposal. Does he or she have any questions or comments? Is there anything this person would like you to explain or clarify? Many of the issues your counterpart raises can be immediately clarified. Potential controversies may be avoided when each party *hears* what the other is thinking. Particular terms can be explained, and possibly offensive language can be modified. By the time the phone call is complete, most of the issues raised have been resolved amicably. Had you not had this telephone conference, however, misunderstandings may have become amplified, leading to escalated proposals through return mail, fax, or e-mail.

NEGOTIATING WITH GOVERNMENT REPRESENTATIVES

We are often forced to negotiate with federal, state, or local government agencies. We may have to obtain approval for modifications to our office building, determine how to file unemployment and social security tax forms for individuals who work for us, get property or income tax information, and so on. Most private sector business people dread bargaining interactions with government agencies, afraid those entities don't have any incentive to deal with us fairly. They have the image of distant bureaucrats who are unwilling to apply their regulations in a reasonable manner.

The reason negotiating with government regulators can be so frustrating is that different value systems are involved. Business firms are driven primarily by the need to make a profit; government agencies operate on a nonprofit basis. Government employees often do not fully appreciate the cost constraints that affect most small and many large businesses.

It is important to appreciate the constraints that affect government officials. They are often under great pressure to resolve disputes through negotiated arrangements. They lack the legal staff needed to litigate many cases, and they try to limit their disputes to major issues.

If individuals try to reason with government representatives and make realistic proposals, they will usually achieve mutual accords. Despite the occasional horror stories we read about in the newspapers or see on television, government officials rarely abuse private sector parties. They know that if they do and it becomes public, they may be in big trouble.

Since profit doesn't motivate government officials, what does influence them? They are enamored of their own rules and regulations. They know their rules completely and have a form for every conceivable situation. If you ever challenge their basic rules, they will fight you all the way to the United States Supreme Court. If you can possibly avoid this situation by trying to fit your circumstances within their existing rules—even if your proposed solution involves a strained construction of their regulations—government negotiators are more likely to give you what you are seeking. Explain to them why it is in their interest to give you what you want. If it seems appropriate, they will usually agree with you.

One especially frustrating aspect of bargaining with government officials is the limited authority possessed by lower government agents. Rarely do department heads provide their subordinates with expansive authority. They know that they will be held politically responsible for decisions made by their agencies, and they limit their underlings' freedom to protect themselves. Their agents normally know what they can sell to their superiors, and they don't enter into agreements they think are unacceptable. They resent it when they are overruled by their superiors. They thus fight for your interests when they seek the approval of higher agency personnel.

Once you reach agreements with government employees, trust their ability to obtain final approval. It is important to give them the information they will need when they meet with higher agency officials. If you don't provide this assistance, you diminish the likelihood that your deal will be accepted. Have faith in the fact that most agreements negotiated by government representatives are ultimately approved by department heads. Since the approval process usually takes time, you must be patient. Don't harass the agency officials until you believe your situation has become completely lost within the bureaucracy. If you push too quickly or too hard, they always have the ability to deny what you are seeking. While you may subsequently be able to get that decision reversed by higher agency officials, this process will be time-consuming and expensive. You are far better off if you can negotiate the appropriate terms with agency employees and help them to obtain the approval of their superiors.

What should you do after your proposed deal has languished within the agency for a prolonged period of time? You should first contact the person with whom you initially interacted and politely ask about the status of your file. He or she may refocus on your matter and get it approved. If you feel that the person with immediate authority over your situation is afraid to make a decision, you may contact the next higher agency official and request that person's assistance. Some bureaucrats are hesitant to make difficult decisions, because they fear retaliation if they make a mistake. They prefer to make no decision, so they are safe. When you encounter such people, first contact them and try to convince them that what you are requesting is not the least bit controversial or inappropriate. Only when this approach fails to generate action should you seek the assistance of higher agency personnel.

SUMMARY POINTS

- Negotiators employ various techniques during the distributive part of bargaining interactions to enable them to claim more of the items being divided between the participants. Some of these techniques include:

  - time pressure
  - dual messages
  - extreme opening offers
  - probing questions
  - flinching or looking dejected
  - nibbling
  - range offers
  - decreasing or limited duration offers
  - anger
  - aggressive behavior
  - walking out/slamming down the telephone
  - Mutt & Jeff (also known as Good Cop/Bad Cop)
  - irrationality (or crazy like a fox)
  - false demands
  - alleged expertise
  - false concessions
  - predicting disaster
  - playing Brer Rabbit
  - going Belly-Up

- By understanding the different bargaining techniques and the appropriate counter-measures, negotiators can decide which tactics to employ and how to neutralize the impact of opponent techniques.

CHAPTER 7

STAGE THREE: THE CLOSING STAGE

If you have made it to the end of the Distributive Stage, you and your bargaining counterparts can safely assume that an agreement is going to be achieved. You experience a sense of relief, pleased that the uncertainty of the negotiating process is about to be replaced by definitive terms—a deal. If you observe carefully, you will see signs of relief around the mouths of everyone at the table. They, and you, will assume more relaxed postures. Once this stage is reached, and all the participants become psychologically committed to final agreement, they often begin to move quickly toward the conclusion of their interaction.

PATIENCE IS CRITICAL

Don't rush to close a deal. A majority of all concessions made during the bargaining encounter are made during this stage. While the concessions themselves are generally smaller than earlier position changes, their total amount can become significant. If you are overly anxious and move too quickly toward final terms, you stand to lose much of what you gained during the distributive stage. It is important that you remain patient and allow the closing stage to develop in a deliberate manner.

When the Closing Stage begins, many bargainers recognize that the conclusion is in sight and speed up, eager to complete the interaction. Instead of being a time for swift action, this is a time for perseverance. Continue using the techniques that took you this far, because those tactics have been successful. Keep the process heading inexorably toward a final accord, and do so patiently. To accomplish this objective, avoid disruptive tactics, such as a walk-out or the slamming down of the telephone. If you break off talks now, you may need days or weeks to return to this point in the transaction if you are able to get back to the table at all.

Be aware of your own concession pattern and that of the other side. Try to make smaller and, if possible, less frequent concessions than your counterparts. If you ignore this recent history and try to reach final terms too quickly, *you* will close most of the distance that still separates you from the other party.

Less proficient negotiators make excessive and consecutive position changes during the Closing Stage in an effort to seal the deal. They are afraid to risk the possibility of impasse at this point in the transaction. They know that the terms to be achieved through settlement will be better than their non-settlement alternatives. They fail to appreciate the fact that their counterparts are feeling the pressure, too. Take your time at this stage, and always remember how much the other side wants to obtain final agreements.

TECHNIQUES YOU CAN USE

By the conclusion of the Distributive Stage, *both sides* have become psychologically committed to agreement. Neither side wants its prior bargaining efforts to culminate in failure. Less proficient participants focus entirely on their own side's desire to achieve final terms, disregarding the settlement pressure impacting their opponents. This causes them to heighten the pressure that influences them, and to discount the anxiety their adversaries are experiencing. They thus feel a need to close more of the gap remaining between the two sides.

By the time the Closing Stage is reached, *both sides* want an agreement. They would not have spent the time and effort needed to get this far if an accord was not preferable to an impasse. Both sides should move together toward the final resolution. Protect the hard work you've done up to this point in the negotiation. Don't make concessions that are not reciprocated by your counterparts. Avoid excessive position changes that are not matched by the other side. Consider larger concessions at this point only when it is clear that your counterparts made greater position changes earlier and seem to be approaching their bottom line.

Skilled bargainers often obtain significant gains during the concluding portions of interactions. A particularly effective technique for the Closing Stage is *the promise technique*. If you want your counterparts to alter their position, use the promise technique (rather than disruptive threats or warnings) to induce them to move in a face-saving way. Indicate your willingness to make another concession if they change their position. You can often overcome temporary impasses by doing this, for your opponents will be likely to make position changes that you have promised to reciprocate.

Patience and *silence* are two of the most powerful devices to use during the Closing Stage. Each time you announce a position change, succinctly indicate the amount and reason for your new offer and become quiet. It is the other side's turn to respond. Say nothing. Continued babble will be perceived as a sign of anxiety and weakness. Don't contemplate further movement without reciprocal movement by the other party, and don't hesitate to remind unyielding opponents of your previous position changes to generate guilt and to convince the other side that it must make the next move.

Intelligent Negotiators often project a *personal indifference* that is designed to scare their counterparts. They want those individuals to think they do not care whether they achieve final accords. The more you can indicate a willingness to walk away if better terms are not forthcoming, the more you can induce opponents to close the remaining gap between you. By getting your counterparts to make larger and more frequent position changes at this stage, you can regain much of what you gave up during the Distributive Stage.

The distance between the parties once they reach the closing stage is not usually large—but it can still be significant. A $1,000 or $5,000 difference is important to someone with limited financial resources. A $50,000 gap is significant to most people, while a $5 million difference is huge to almost everyone. When overly anxious participants give up most of the $1,000, $5,000, $50,000, or $5 million gap, they regret their unnecessary generosity. If they patiently allow the Closing Stage to develop, they can increase the probability that their side will obtain more of the remaining gap.

I have often seen impatient negotiators give up thousands of dollars during the final minutes of the Closing Stage to guarantee agreements. In some instances, I have seen people concede hundreds of thousands of dollars—and occasionally even millions of dollars—near the end of bargaining encounters. I can recall a corporate sales transaction involving a $1 billion business deal. Near the end of the interaction, the parties were about $30 million apart. The negotiators broke off talks to consult their respective principals. The buyer concluded that he should have accepted the seller's proposal, and decided to call the seller first thing in the morning to accept his offer. The buyer did just that, but the seller interrupted before the buyer could accept. The seller rushed in to say that he should not have let the buyer leave the evening before, and agreed to accept the buyer's last offer—closing the entire $30 million gap. The call recipient (the seller) apparently feared that the buyer was thinking of withdrawing his last offer, and quickly accepted the buyer's outstanding proposal from the previous day, before the buyer, who initiated the telephone call could change his mind. Had the seller been more patient when receiving the phone call, he would have gained millions of dollars.

At this stage of the process, you must remember to look across the bargaining table and ask how much *your counterparts* want or need the deal. Your opponents usually want to achieve final terms as much as you do—and they may be more anxious to do so in some situations. Ignore this likelihood, and you will concede all your bargaining power to your counterparts.

WRAPPING UP

Despite the seemingly cooperative aspect of the Closing Stage, this is a highly competitive portion of the interaction. It involves a substantial number of position changes. Negotiators who do not ensure reciprocal movement by their counterparts may lose their hard-won gains. Do not succumb to your counterparts' efforts to get you to close most of the remaining gap, thereby causing you to accept inferior terms. Always remember how much your *opponents* desire an agreement. If you keep this firmly in mind as you close the deal, you should be able to induce the other side to make the concessions needed to solidify the deal.

Near the very end of the Closing Stage, there is often a small gap remaining between the participants. Both sides are certain that an agreement is going to be achieved, but who should make the final concession? If you are an adversarial negotiator, you will probably try to induce your counterparts to close the remaining distance. This approach may provide you with a slight monetary gain, but it may also leave your counterparts with negative feelings. If you two have future dealings, those negotiators who were forced to make the last concession may be out for revenge. Both Innovators and Cooperatives recognize the goodwill to be generated by final position changes on their part. This cooperative gesture leaves your counterparts with the sense that they got a good deal, a psychological benefit that will likely outweigh the relatively insignificant monetary concession involved. It also creates a positive negotiating environment that should enhance the cooperative discussions that are to follow.

The closing stage of Felicia's employment negotiations proceeds slowly and steadily, despite her temptation to rush things.

Felicia informs Solomon that she is still concerned about two issues. She asks whether President Andersen might consider a slightly higher starting salary. Solomon wants to know whether she would accept $62,000 if he could get President Andersen's approval. When Felicia responds affirmatively, he promises to request such approval. Felicia then says that she would like to know how much the firm would be willing to pay each year for training programs. When Solomon proposes a $5,000 limit, she says this would be acceptable. He says how pleased he is to have Felicia joining the firm.

Felicia finally tells Solomon that she would find it difficult to begin full-time work within the next two months. Solomon asks if she might be able to begin within six weeks, and she indicates that she could probably do so.

SUMMARY POINTS

- The Closing Stage is marked by developing certainty, relaxation, and increased commitment to final agreement.

- Participants should move steadily toward a successful conclusion, but never rush the process. Keep your opponents' desire for final agreement firmly in mind.

- Effective techniques include promises, patience, silence, and feigned indifference.

- Near the end of interactions, negotiators must be patient and avoid unreciprocated concessions.

CHAPTER 8

STAGE FOUR: THE COOPERATIVE STAGE

The Closing Stage has been successfully completed. You and your counterparts have agreed upon mutually acceptable terms. Many negotiators now consider the bargaining process completed. It is *not* finished. This conclusion may be warranted (but not always) with respect to interactions that involve only the immediate payment of money (in which case neither participant could gain without a corresponding loss by the other side); but it is not correct when multi-issue interactions are involved. Once the Closing Stage ends, you enter Stage Four, the cooperative stage, also called Maximizing the Joint Return. Intelligent Negotiators take this opportunity to expand the pie and seek the most efficient distribution of items. You should use this stage to go beyond "acceptable terms" and improve the returns for both parties.

While many bargaining interactions appear to involve only monetary transfers that include no room for cooperative exchanges, some of these can be modified to permit joint gains. For example, in a home sale negotiation, the current owners believe they should get $250,000, but the prospective buyers can only afford $230,000. The sellers might agree to carry a $20,000 personal loan that the buyers will pay off over the next ten years, which will enable the purchasers to pay the full $250,000 price. The sellers would also get the benefit of the interest on that loan over the ten-year period. Or, in another cooperative bargaining scenario, the buyers may have a contracting business that will enable them to pay $230,000 in cash and promise to provide $25,000 in contracting services for the sellers in the new house they plan to buy across town. The sellers receive $230,000 plus $25,000 in services, resulting in their receiving a selling "price" of $255,000. Providing the additional services may only cost the buyers $15,000, resulting in their paying a purchasing "price" of $245,000. In both of these situations, the buyers and the sellers obtain what they want, despite the fact that their initial positions seemed irreconcilable.

Other situations involve much higher stakes. For example, a company that wants to purchase another firm lacks the cash to pay the $50 million asking price. The purchasing party may offer $40 million in cash and $10 million in stock, or may alternatively offer $35 million in cash and $15 million in goods or services it knows the selling firm wants that it can provide. The selling firm values those goods and services at the $15 million they would have to pay to buy those items, while the purchaser values them at the $9 million it costs them to generate the items.

Cooperative bargaining is most natural when individuals become involved in bargaining interactions that include a number of different items. This is so because both sides do not place equal value on the same items. Although we often assume that they do, this assumption is rarely correct. One party prefers to obtain certain items, while the other hopes to get other terms. It is thus entirely possible for negotiators to formulate proposals that simultaneously advance the interests of both sides. Let's look at how to do this.

GOING BEYOND ACCEPTABLE TERMS: THE SEARCH FOR UNDISCOVERED ALTERNATIVES

During the Distributive and the Closing Stages, the participants often behave disingenuously to advance their own selfish interests. They may, for example, overstate or understate the value of items being exchanged for strategic purposes. Both you and your counterpart want to convince the other that what you are giving up is substantial, while what you are getting is not. Sellers of products or services embellish the value of those items, while purchasers of those goods or services devalue their significance. Because of these manipulative tactics, truly efficient agreements—where neither party may improve its position without worsening the other side's circumstances—are often not attained. The parties merely achieve "acceptable" terms, without even considering the possibility that they could generate more beneficial agreements for *both sides*. If you conclude your interaction at this point, you may leave a substantial amount of potential, yet untapped joint satisfaction on the bargaining table.

To go beyond acceptable terms, you and your counterparts need to explore alternative trade-offs that may concurrently enhance the interests of both sides. This is best done after a tentative agreement has been achieved through the Distributive and Closing Stages. Even if you are mentally exhausted due to the extended negotiations, take a few minutes to explore alternative formulations that may prove to be mutually beneficial. What you are looking for are items that ended on the wrong side of the bargaining table—the items the conceding party actually valued more highly than the side receiving those terms.

For example, two spouses may be discussing the terms for their marital dissolution. They have tentatively agreed to joint custody of their two children, given the primary residence to one and the vacation home to the other. One got the one-year-old convertible, while the other got the two-year-old sport utility vehicle. If they were to finalize these terms, they may not maximize their joint return. For example, the husband may be willing to give the wife sole custody, if he received generous visitation rights. The wife may be willing to give up her claim to the principal residence if she could sell the vacation home and use the proceeds to purchase a new house near the schools both parents want the children to attend. The wife, because she would be getting custody, may prefer the SUV rather than the convertible, due to the ease with which she could use that vehicle to transport the children. If the couple never contemplated these possible trade-offs, they would part company with far less than they could obtain through efficient cooperative bargaining.

Getting Your Basic Agreement in Place First

If the Cooperative Stage is to be used effectively, you must first reach a tentative agreement on which topics are available for distribution and how those items should be divided. If your counterpart tries to convince you that the Distributive or Closing Stage is unnecessary and suggests that you eschew all but cooperative win-win tactics, he is probably trying to preempt the interaction and win the Distributive Stage by default. He will succeed in his plan if you go along with his suggestions. For if these matters are not set in the Distributive and Closing Stages, your counterpart will be able to dictate the basic division of the available topics. He will also be able to use the Cooperative Stage to obtain a further advantage. Do not let this happen. It is thus imperative that negotiators participate in effective Distributive and Closing Stages *before* they move into the Cooperative Stage.

Initiating Cooperative Bargaining

Once tentative terms have been agreed upon, you can suggest exploration of the Cooperative Stage. If you fear that your counterparts might be reluctant to move in this direction, take the following steps:

1. Draft a written document and have the parties initial each term agreed upon to signify their concurrence in the overall agreement.

2. Propose the joint exploration of alternative formulations that may prove to be mutually beneficial but were overlooked during the prior stages of the interaction.

Be sure that both sides recognize your transition from the Closing Stage to the Cooperative Stage. If one side tries to move into the Cooperative Stage too quickly without the understanding of the other party, the whole deal may unravel. When the cooperative bargainer begins to suggest alternative proposals, they may be less advantageous to the other side than the previously agreed upon terms. If the recipient of these new proposals does not understand these to be incipient cooperative offers, he or she may suspect manipulative tactics and accuse the cooperative bargainer of bad faith negotiating. Once this happens, the entire interaction may break down. This is why the party making the first move into the Cooperative Stage should be sure the other side understands what is taking place.

Look for Mutually Beneficial Tradeoffs

Keep in mind your primary goal: to expand the overall economic and non-economic pie to be divided between you and your counterpart. To achieve this, you must do all you can to ascertain the presence of previously unnoticed alternatives that go beyond the merely acceptable, and improve both sides' respective situations. Contemplate options that would more effectively satisfy the underlying interests of your counterpart with less cost to you, and vice-versa. To accomplish this goal, both sides must be willing to candidly disclose their underlying interests. You and your counterparts can no longer directly over- or understate the value of items for strategic reasons. You must indicate what you truly hope to obtain and explain why you prefer those terms.

Through an objective exploration of the underlying needs and interests of the parties, you and your counterpart can look for areas in which you may generate joint gains. Each of you must indicate what you in fact hope to accomplish and then both engage in brainstorming to develop options that were not previously considered. When your counterpart asks you whether a different formulation would be as good or better for you than what was already agreed upon, you must be forthright. If the proposed trade would not be preferable, the participants should contemplate other options. How else might they better satisfy the underlying needs of each? What other formulations may prove to be mutually advantageous?

The managing partner of a business firm may have just offered someone a new position with a $60,000 salary, a compensation level that might initially be insufficient to lure the prospective employee away from her current situation. The offering company may not wish to increase the starting salary; it may, however, be willing to offer the person a five-year guaranteed employment contract, or promise her advancement opportunities not available with her current employer. The company may agree to cover the cost of specialized training or advanced education that would enhance the skills of the new hire and make her more valuable to the hiring firm. It may agree to reassess her salary after her first six months on the job. Through such win-win exchanges, the negotiators may improve the value of the deal to both sides.

You and your counterpart must try to preserve your basic credibility as you enter the Cooperative Stage. Both sides may have used puffing and embellishment early in the negotiation, during the Information Exchange and the Distributive and Closing Stages, to deceive each other. Regard the Cooperative Stage as a place to correct the inefficiencies that may have been generated by these deceptive tactics. If you are too candid about your previous misrepresentations, however, your counterparts may begin to question the validity of other claims you have made and attempt to renegotiate the entire deal. This could cause the interaction to break down. Be careful not to overtly undermine your credibility while you are exploring alternative formulations during the Cooperative Stage.

It is important for any negotiator participating in cooperative bargaining to appreciate the competitive undercurrent that may affect even these discussions. When cooperating participants discover areas for joint gain, nothing requires them to share that gain on an equal basis. If your counterpart offers you a much better arrangement, move slowly. Do not directly acknowledge how much this arrangement benefits you. Your counterpart is unlikely to appreciate how much that offer would improve your circumstances. Simply indicate that you would prefer these terms to the prior arrangement. In doing this, you avoid having to give him as much as you would have to provide if he realized how much of a concession he was actually proposing. Remember how competitive this exchange is. If you offer the other side more beneficial terms, be sure that your concessions are reciprocated by your counterpart.

When Agreement Is Achieved, Review Basic Terms and Draft Accord

The Cooperative Stage ends when you and your counterparts have a mutual accord. Before you part company or hang up the telephone, briefly review the terms you think have been agreed upon to be certain there has really been a meeting of the minds. Mention all the different terms you have included. In most cases, this process will confirm what you think you have agreed upon. On a few occasions, however, you may encounter some misunderstandings. Now, when both sides are psychologically committed to settlement, is the time to identify them so that you and your counterparts can resolve them amicably. If you did not discover them for several weeks, the discovering party may raise claims of bad faith and accuse the other side of dishonesty.

At the end of many bargaining encounters, the parties have to write up their agreement in a relatively formal document. Whenever possible, take the opportunity to prepare the written summary of your agreement. You have to believe that you will do a better job of representing your own interests than would those with whom you are negotiating. I would not for a moment suggest that you ever contemplate changing what has been agreed upon when you draft the actual accord. Not only would this be completely unethical, but you would be exposing yourself to claims of fraud, and your reputation as a negotiator could be destroyed.

On rare occasions you may encounter counterparts who, when drafting written agreements, deliberately change what the parties have agreed upon. To avoid these problems, always review carefully the specific terms of any draft your adversaries prepare to be sure it reflects what you think it should. You are examining that document to verify three things:

1. *Do you like language they have included?* If not, don't hesitate to take out a pen or pencil and mark up the draft. If they try to thwart your review efforts by complaining about the total number of changes you are requesting, ask them to send you the computer disk containing their draft and offer to make the requisite modifications. They will refuse to provide you with their disk, but will cease their complaining.

2. *Is there any provision in that document that you don't recall discussing?* Some drafters include "boilerplate" language they think will offend no one. While they should highlight such provisions to alert you to their inclusion, some drafters inadvertently fail to do so. Remember that nothing is "boilerplate" until both sides agree that it is. Be sure they are not including a clause that may disadvantage you in the future. For example, in a new employment contract, the hiring firm may have included a provision requiring all controversies to be resolved through binding arbitration procedures controlled by the hiring company. If you were to sign a contract containing such a clause, you may be unable to seek judicial relief if you later thought you were discriminated against in violation of state or federal civil rights laws or were terminated unjustly for refusing to engage in conduct that violated an important state or federal public policy.

3. *Has anything that you think was agreed upon been omitted?* This is the most difficult task of all, because most individuals reviewing a written document look for what has been included rather than what may have been excluded. If we like what is there, we fail to appreciate what may not be there. As you review the included provisions, check off your notes pertaining to those areas. When you are finished, look to see whether there is anything in your notes that has not been reflected in the draft contract.

What should you do when you suspect disingenuous drafting by counterparts? You might contact them and challenge their integrity, but they would undoubtedly deny dishonesty and the whole deal may unravel. This is especially true if their mistakes were inadvertent and they resent your challenge to their honesty. It is more effective to contact your counterparts, point out the areas in question, and ask them to review their notes pertaining to those areas. In most instances, you will discover that either you or your counterparts have made honest mistakes that can be quickly corrected. Even if your counterparts have deliberately tried to cheat you, by raising the issue in this manner you provide them with a face-saving way out. They can apologize and correct the "erroneous" provisions.

Tit-for-Tat

A number of years ago, Professor Robert Axelrod decided to conduct a competitive exercise on computers using the so-called "Prisoner's Dilemma."[1] In this game, two prisoners are allegedly caught by the police and interrogated separately. The police do not have clear evidence of their guilt, thus they hope to induce one to become a witness against the other. Each choice a prisoner makes, whether it is to confess or to remain silent, is referred to in the game as an *iteration*. If one agrees to cooperate but the other does not, the cooperating person gets a short jail term (six months, for example) while the other gets a more substantial term (say, ten years). If both confess, they both get moderate terms (five years), while if neither confesses they both get shorter terms (two years). If the game players experiment with a number of iterations, they find they maximize their joint return by refusing to cooperate with the police. In this scenario they each get two years for each iteration. On the other hand, if one confesses while the other does not, the confessor gets a short term and their partner gets a long term. While it might thus seem optimal to confess, if both do so, each one gets an intermediate term.

Professor Anatol Rapoport entered a program called "Tit-for-Tat," in which his prisoner would remain silent on the first iteration and on each subsequent iteration would do exactly what the other side's programmed prisoner did on the preceding iteration. Although Professor Rapoport's program never beat the other side (the best it did was tie with that program), his program prevailed over all the others. When his program lost, it lost by so little that over the entire competition it achieved the best cumulative results.

From the Prisoner's Dilemma experiment, Professor Rapoport developed some rules designed to encourage others to behave cooperatively when they interact with you.[2] Intelligent Negotiators who use these Tit-for-Tat guidelines in the cooperative stage will obtain the best possible results.

> *First: Don't be envious of your opponent's results.*
> Don't be a win-lose negotiator who judges your success by how poorly your opponents have done, but rather be a win-win negotiator who asks whether you are pleased with what you got. If you got a good deal, that fact that your counterpart is also pleased should not detract from the gains you have achieved.

> *Second: Always begin with a cooperative attitude.*
> Never plan to employ inappropriate behavior of an adversarial nature. This positive approach is likely to encourage similar cooperation from others.

Third: Fight back when you encounter inappropriately adversarial behavior. Politely but forcefully lean back on those who use overtly competitive tactics. Make it clear you will not let them take advantage of you. If someone uses the Nibble Technique (see chapter 6) to seize items from you at the conclusion of an interaction, be sure to demand reciprocity for what they are seeking instead of merely giving in to their one-sided demands.

Fourth: Be forgiving. Never hold a grudge. Don't take the negotiation process personally. Once you have challenged your opponent's improper conduct, make it clear you plan to cooperate with that person in the future as long as they continue to cooperate with you.

Fifth: Establish an appropriate reputation. Through your interactions with others, establish a reputation as a cooperative negotiator who will respond appropriately to counteract improper conduct by overly competitive adversaries. Others will learn of your reputation and think twice before they resort to hostile behavior.

Felicia actively seeks alternative approaches during the Cooperative Stage of her negotiation with Andersen.

Before Felicia and Solomon part company, she asks whether the firm would increase her signing bonus instead of reimbursing her for moving expenses. She realizes that anything Andersen provides with respect to moving expenses will cause an equal reduction in the amount her husband is reimbursed by the State EPA. Solomon suggests a $2,000 increase in her $1,000 signing bonus, which she readily accepts.

When Solomon asks Felicia if she could possibly begin work in four weeks instead of six, she seems reluctant. He finally asks if she could begin on a part-time basis in four weeks and go to full-time four weeks thereafter. She indicates that she could probably work twenty-five hours per week during that four-week transition period, and he looks pleased. He then graciously says that if she is willing to accept the earlier starting date on a part-time basis, he would ensure that she is paid on a full-time basis as soon as she initially begins her part-time work.

SUMMARY POINTS

- Through cooperative efforts, negotiators can expand the pie to be divided and simultaneously improve their respective situations.

- Get your bargaining agreement in place before you enter the Cooperative Stage.

- Cooperative bargaining may be beneficial for even pure money exchanges, as parties use in-kind and future payments to enhance their joint interests.

- When multiple item negotiations are involved, the participants should seek to go beyond the acceptable, actively exploring alternative options with the goal of maximizing the joint return through the most efficient distribution of the items being exchanged.

- When agreements are achieved, negotiators should briefly review the basic terms and attempt to draft the final accords.

- Intelligent Negotiators use the "Tit-for-Tat" approach to encourage opponents to engage in cooperative behavior.

PART IV

FREQUENTLY ENCOUNTERED NEGOTIATING SITUATIONS

CHAPTER 9

SITUATION 1: NEGOTIATING EMPLOYMENT OPPORTUNITIES

The paths to initial employment and subsequent advancement consist of a series of critical negotiations. If you are seeking either a new position or advancement at your present job, view these situations as Intelligent Negotiating opportunities. This approach will give you an edge you can use to build your career.

NEW POSITIONS

The first negotiation is to secure an interview. When you learn of an available position, you usually contact the firm directly or go through a university or private placement office. You have to make a good impression with those scheduling interviews and convince them that you deserve an interview. If you are rude or seem incompetent, they may indicate that all interview slots are filled. On the other hand, even if the interviewer's schedule is full, if you make an especially good impression, the scheduler is likely to fit you in during the day, or at the beginning or end of the interview schedule.

Many businesses advertise positions with only an e-mail address so that you must approach them by e-mail. If this is the case with the job you want, send a professional resume and cover letter, and after a week or two has passed, follow up with a polite note to the original contact, making sure they received the resume.

Prepare Thoroughly

When you do reach someone by telephone, or go in person to ask about a vacant position you are interested in, be fully prepared for that preliminary encounter. Read the available job announcement carefully to be sure you know what the job entails and what the expected qualifications are. Have a professional resume with you, in case the scheduler asks for a copy. Be prepared to describe your personal qualifications, if asked. The scheduler may possess the authority to determine who will be considered at all, thus you want to make a good impression on that person. You may also show up at the personnel office to schedule an interview and be asked to meet with the interviewer at that time. If you are prepared for such a possibility, you will make a better showing than if you are unprepared.

If you get on the interviewer's schedule, prepare for that encounter. Be sure to wear proper attire—clothing appropriate for someone applying for the position you are seeking. When in doubt, keep in mind that you are better off overdressed than underdressed. Even if the firm in question has "casual Fridays" and you are scheduled for a Friday session, dress in the same manner you would for an interview on another day of the week. While the interviewer may be wearing casual clothing, he or she is likely to expect *you* to dress more formally.

The Initial Interview

The preliminary portion of your meeting with the interviewer is especially important. Studies show that most interviewers form an initial impression during the first minute or two they spend with you. They then use the remaining portion of the interview trying to confirm their initial impression. It is thus crucial to begin your encounter in a highly professional manner. Introduce yourself politely but forcefully, and shake hands firmly with the interviewer. If she begins the small talk standing up, you should remain standing. Take a seat when she asks you to or when she elects to do so.

Be prepared to explain why you should be given the job. What are your specific qualifications? What unique personal skills could you bring to this firm? What other full- or part-time positions have you held that have prepared you for this type of employment? You may be asked about your specific strengths and weaknesses. Try to use these questions as opportunities to sell yourself. Emphasize your capabilities, and minimize your weaknesses. If asked about your weaknesses, try not to use clichés such as "I work too hard" or "I am overly conscientious." Be honest, but don't emphasize your negative traits.

Don't hesitate to ask questions of the interviewer. If the job description contains general language, ask about the specific job functions involved. Don't hesitate to ask about advancement opportunities with the firm, because this demonstrates both a long-term interest and personal ambition. Try not to ask specific questions about salary and benefits at this stage of the selection process. The interviewer is likely to consider such inquiries presumptuous of someone who has not been offered the position. She should provide you with enough general information regarding these matters to satisfy your current interests. It is beneficial to use questions to get the interviewer talking. The more she speaks and you demonstrate active listening skills, the more likely she will be able to evaluate you favorably.

Salary Discussions

Avoid specific salary discussions until after you are offered a position. If the interviewer asks you about your salary requirements, attempt to provide a general—rather than a specific—response. You could mention your present salary, but may feel more comfortable responding with a question concerning the range for the position you are seeking. If you provide a specific answer and the number you cite is considered high, this may undermine the likelihood you will get the job. On the other hand, if you mention an unusually low number, the interviewer may think something is wrong with you. Why would someone with your capabilities be willing to accept such meager compensation? In addition, should you ultimately be offered the position at the low salary you mentioned, you may become a bitter and dissatisfied employee. If you are asked about your present compensation level and think it doesn't reflect your personal value, don't hesitate to describe the skills you possess that make you worth more than you are currently earning. You can also indicate that you are looking for a more challenging position that will provide you with greater opportunities for advancement.

During the interview process, the business firm possesses the bargaining power. The firm has the job you want, as well as a number of qualified applicants. During this stage, those responsible for hiring are merely deciding which applicants to reject and which to consider. If you give them a reason (such as excessive salary expectations) to exclude you, they will do so. On the other hand, if you provide them with reasons to warrant consideration, you are likely to get to the next level. It is thus important to focus on the reasons for your inclusion, and avoid discussion of issues that may cause your disqualification.

Your bargaining power as a job applicant increases with the more expertise you have in a particular field or industry. Over time, you continue to garner more skills, contacts, and accomplishments, so you become increasingly more valuable as a seasoned performer who has already proven yourself in a specific arena.

The Compensation Package

Once you successfully negotiate your way through the selection process and obtain a firm offer, the balance of bargaining power shifts in your direction. The firm has decided to employ you, and the hiring official wants to secure your acceptance. This is the time to ask specific questions about salary and benefits.

Through friends, placement offices, trade groups, and other sources, you should have already obtained information concerning the compensation levels pertaining to positions of this type. If you have Internet access, you can use sites such as www.jobsmart.org to gain information about relevant salary surveys that have been conducted recently. You can also find salary listings for various positions at sites such as www.hotjobs.com.

If possible, get the hiring person to make the initial offer by asking about the usual salary for this position. Even if the number mentioned is acceptable to you, don't hesitate to politely ask: "Is this the best figure you can offer?" Personnel officers generally begin with lower offers and expect job candidates to bargain for higher salaries. They may ultimately provide you with a more generous offer that will benefit you for the entire time you are with this firm. If they reply that this is the compensation level for this job, you may be able to modify their offer by suggesting any unique personal skills you possess that will enhance your value to the firm. You may also ask whether the firm would be willing to reconsider the compensation level in six months, after they have had the chance to observe your work.

The hiring person will normally provide you with a brochure describing the fringe benefits available to firm employees. Review the benefits package carefully. Be sure it includes the health coverage, retirement plan, and other options you and your family need. Don't be afraid to ask whether there are other fringe benefits the firm might cover completely or include with supplemental premiums that you pay. If you are already covered under your spouse's health plan, you might be able to trade other benefits or a higher salary if you were to forego this firm's health insurance.

If you would like to obtain additional perks, such as flexible work hours, reimbursement for professional dues, travel to conferences and conventions, reimbursement for external training courses, or free or subsidized parking, include these on a list with several other more expensive items you don't expect to get (a company car or a large corner office, for example). This enables the firm to offer you the extra terms you are seeking, while rejecting the items they consider inappropriate. They are pleased that you yielded on those terms, and you leave with the items you really hoped to obtain.

Specifics of the Position

Ask about the specific requirements of the job being offered. What are the exact job responsibilities involved? Is travel required and how much of it? Does the firm provide employees with special training classes or pay for the cost of professional development courses you may need to take from external institutions? What advancement opportunities should be available to qualified individuals? Can you anticipate regular reviews of your performance and of your compensation level? Can you expect continued employment if your performance is exemplary?

In the United States, almost all private sector employees are retained on an "at will" basis. Under this system, both the employer and the worker can terminate their relationship at any time for any reason that does not violate specific laws (such a civil rights statutes prohibiting discrimination). If you can get a prospective employer to tell you that you can expect future employment for as long as your work is good, this may provide you with some protection beyond "at will" coverage. A firm that has made such a specific promise would be hesitant to terminate you without a valid reason. It is particularly beneficial to obtain promises of this type in writing to protect your future interests. In many cases, this information is bundled into the huge amount of information in the human resource manuals that are given to new employees.

Once you have obtained the answers to your questions, you must decide whether or not to accept the employer's offer. Is the firm offering you an opportunity that is consistent with your professional goals? Be aware of the impact of *psychological entrapment* and be sure you are not seeking this position solely because you have not been able to find other positions you really want. If you have been looking for other employment for a number of months and this is the first offer you have received, carefully compare this opportunity with your present circumstances. Would it really improve your personal situation? If not, stay where you are and keep looking for appropriate opportunities. Never take a new job simply because it is available.

PAY INCREASES

Once you have an acceptable job, how should you seek compensation increases? Do not make the mistake of asking your superiors for salary raises based on your personal needs. Many employees do this, by saying that they want to purchase a larger house, their children are going to expensive private schools or colleges, or they have to provide financial assistance for their ailing parents. Company officers are rarely moved by such arguments. Business firms are not charitable organizations; they are primarily motivated by a desire to make money. Employers don't advance their profit-maximizing objective by giving their employees the money to buy new homes, educate their children, or take care of aging parents; they pay compensation for what employees bring to the organization.

When you seek a salary increase, you have to provide your superior with reasons *the firm* should want to improve your compensation level. You can cite the dollar amount of new business you have brought in to the company since your last raise, the improvements you've made in existing systems, or the successful implementation of a valuable new program, to name a few. Prepare for the impending interaction as thoroughly as you would any other important bargaining encounter. Gather relevant information from coworkers and personnel at similar companies. Economic data may be available from newspapers, magazines, trade publications, and Internet sites. The more information you have supporting your requested raise, the more likely you are to be successful.

If your firm has regular performance reviews, you can bring up the matter of a salary increase at the time you are preparing for the review. If possible, put it in writing. If you are not anticipating a review, try to select a propitious time to ask for the desired increase. If your superior has been extremely busy lately, wait until things calm down if possible. It may be beneficial to wait until the firm issues positive financial information indicating increased revenues. Try to schedule a personal meeting at his or her office or your office so that you will have his or her undivided attention. It is exceedingly difficult to discuss your particular request with a supervisor who is simultaneously taking phone calls or conducting unrelated business at the same time you are stating your case.

In the meeting, mention the work you have already performed. You could also detail your current skills—and those you have recently acquired through special courses or advanced education. Mention that you are planning to enhance your skills in the coming months, if this is so. Have you accepted additional responsibilities that make you more valuable to the firm? Would you be willing to accept new responsibilities if this would enable you to advance within the organization? The answers to these questions will be especially important if you are already being paid what comparable employees are earning, because you have to demonstrate the greater personal potential that warrants a higher salary. You have to establish why *you* are important to your employer.

If you have learned that comparable employees at this firm are being paid higher salaries, casually mention this factor. Most businesses try to maintain equitable compensation levels among employees performing similar work. They may not realize that you have fallen behind your colleagues. This can be particularly useful for you if you initially accepted a salary in the lower end of the firm's salary spectrum and are now hoping to eliminate this existing inequity. If you have learned that competitor firms are paying their employees higher salaries for similar jobs, this may also support your request. When you mention compensation levels at other companies, be careful not to state this information so affirmatively that your superior suggests you look for work elsewhere.

Always state your reasons for a requested salary increase positively. Never suggest that the firm is treating you unfairly or is behaving irresponsibly. Superiors rarely appreciate such criticism from their subordinates. State your case in terms of the reasons *you deserve* an increase. This is more likely to generate the desired response. Some supervisors attempt to dodge dealing with pay increase requests by refusing to provide definitive responses to raise requests. If this occurs, ask when you can expect to receive an answer to your inquiry. If your supervisor does not give you a specific date, ask to schedule another meeting at which you can discuss his or her decision.

What should you do if you are only given part of your requested increase? Politely ask if there might be additional room for movement by the firm. If not, ask whether your superior would be willing to reassess the situation within a certain amount of time, such as six months. Don't hesitate to ask what else you could do in terms of your job responsibilities and/or professional development that would increase your chances for advancement within the company. Tell your superior how much you enjoy the opportunity to work at this firm, and indicate your eagerness for personal growth. You might show initiative and team spirit by suggesting that your supervisor tie future compensation increases to the performance of your department or of the firm. Never threaten to move to another company if your requested increase is not approved—unless you are truly prepared to change employers. You never know when the firm will call your bluff and let you go.

Nothing makes an employee appear more valuable than offers from other organizations. If you decide to explore external job opportunities, be careful not to so offend your current employer that he or she decides to get rid of you, the disloyal employee. Approach other companies discreetly. Ask them not to contact your present firm unless absolutely necessary. If you are approached by your superior about rumors that you have been talking to other companies, never lie about the matter. Indicate that you are happy in your present circumstances, but are desirous of greater professional opportunities. This is the perfect time to ask whether you might be given greater responsibilities in your current position. If you make it clear that you would prefer to remain with your immediate employer but hope to improve your situation, you may obtain the opportunities you desire.

Even when you decide to leave a current employer for another, never burn your past bridges. Explain what a difficult decision it is and how much you will miss your present employer. If appropriate to your position, write an exit memo emphasizing these points as well as the positive aspects of your work experience at this company. You never know when you might become dissatisfied with your new position and contemplate a return to your former employer. In addition, in future years, you may require references from your current firm. If you depart in a negative manner, you would be likely to receive less generous recommendations than you would if you left in a pleasant way. Consider also the possibility that your current superior or your co-workers may eventually leave this firm and relocate to other companies for which you would love to work. If you are remembered fondly and are able to stay in touch with key allies as you build your career, you may get a call that could lead to further advancement.

Summary Points

- The paths to employment and advancement involve a series of critical negotiations.
- You must negotiate effectively to obtain a job interview.
- Every employment interview is a negotiation, and prepared candidates do better than unprepared applicants.
- Create a good first impression with interviewers.
- Avoid the discussion of specific salary demands before you are offered the position. After you receive a job offer, you are in a good position to negotiate salary because the firm wants to hire the person it has selected.
- When you seek pay increases, the onus is on you to convince your employer that you are worth more money.
- Be careful not to burn bridges when you leave any firm, and make the effort to stay in touch with key allies as you build your career.

CHAPTER 10

SITUATION 2:
BUYING CARS
AND HOUSES

C ar and house purchases are two of the most significant financial negotiations most people under-
take. Yet, despite the enormous costs involved,
many consumers enter into these bargaining encounters
unprepared. Lack of preparation is the primary reason
these encounters are often unpleasant. The average
buyer approaches car- and house-buying transactions
with two reasons for dreading the encounter:

1. He or she is lacking definitive price information.

2. He or she knows that car salespeople and real estate agents are not working to protect his or her interests. The second factor can rarely be helped. Car
   dealers generally want to sell cars for the highest
   prices possible, just as most real estate agents, who
   are usually working for the home sellers, hope to
   obtain generous terms for those individuals.

The first factor, however, *can* change.

Prospective car and house buyers would do better if they had a better understanding of the selling process and knew how to determine the true values of the items they were purchasing. They would also save substantial sums of money by avoiding excessive deals. Instead of viewing these interactions as unpleasant, they might even look forward to them. After all, isn't it nice to obtain a new car or a new home—both of which should enhance our enjoyment of life?

BUYING NEW CARS

The first thing you must determine is which vehicles would suit your particular needs. Are you looking for a minivan that can carry a number of people and lots of luggage, or a sports car, or a plain sedan? What make or makes of car are you willing to consider? The more flexible you are in these areas, the more walk-away power you will possess when you visit specific dealers. If you absolutely have to have a Chevrolet Corvette or a particular Mercedes, your buying options will be limited. On the other hand, if you would be pleased with a Honda Accord, a Toyota Camry, or a Ford Taurus, you can afford to be bold when you negotiate with dealers because of the many sources available to you.

Determine Dealer Cost

Once you have decided on the vehicle(s) that would satisfy your needs, you must determine the dealer cost for those cars. Car dealers almost never give you this information. They always cite the Manufacturer's Suggested Retail Price (MSRP) set forth on the sheet attached to a side window. They know that if they can anchor this figure in your mind, they can induce you to pay too much. Where can you obtain the information you need? There are various reputable sources you can use. You can visit your local library or bookstore where you will find several books (such as *Kelley Blue Book*) that contain dealer cost information pertaining to all current car models. These will tell you the base dealer cost and the dealer cost for all the popular options you may be considering. You can also obtain the relevant information through the Internet. If you access www.autobytel.com, you can gain entry into the Edmunds Buying Service (www.edmunds.com) that lists the dealer cost for the different vehicles and the available options. You can also go into the *Kelley Blue Book* database (www.kbb.com) and obtain the same information. For a fee of $12.00, you can telephone the Consumer Reports New Car Price Service at (800) 933-5555 and obtain the dealer cost for the exact vehicle and options you desire. These services also try to provide you with current information regarding dealer "holdbacks," usually 2 to 4 percent of dealer cost, which dealers earn from the manufacturer if they sell their vehicles within specified time frames. You must try to determine what manufacturer rebates are being given to their local dealers. These may be reflected in publicly announced rebate programs, or they may be highly confidential. They may amount to hundreds and even thousands of dollars. You also want, if possible, to learn about manufacturer incentives given to dealers who exceed specified sales quotas. These may provide dealers with hundreds of dollars in profit when they appear to be selling vehicles at actual dealer cost. Online services try to estimate the relevant dealer rebates and incentives.

Never make the mistake of allowing car dealers to establish their cost bases through their "invoices." Invoices rarely reflect the actual dealer cost of vehicles. They are a mere approximation of what the dealer was charged when they ordered the vehicle several months ago. They do not include such critical factors as manufacturer rebates to dealers, manufacturer incentives, and dealer holdbacks. These may decrease actual dealer cost by $1,000 to $5,000 or more. Whenever dealers take out their "invoices" to show you how little, if anything, they are making on the proposed sale of the car you want, hold on to your wallet. You are about to be taken in a big way. This is why television and newspaper advertisements stating that dealers will show you their invoice sheets contain small print indicating that "invoices may not reflect actual dealer cost."

Car Negotiating: First Round

Once you have obtained the critical information about dealer cost on the car you want, you can begin to negotiate. When you open buying discussions, salespeople always try to emphasize the MSRP. They want you to focus on that figure to induce you to think how much you are "saving" when they offer you a lower price. Ignore that figure entirely, and change the focus to the dealer cost. State the base cost of the vehicle you are considering and suggest an appropriate dealer profit of from $250 to $750, depending on the demand for the vehicle you are considering. Dealers will usually sell high-volume vehicles for $250 to $350 over their cost, but expect $650 to $750 over cost for low-volume specialized vehicles. The salesperson will look pained and deny the size of your projected manufacturer rebate or incentive or the availability of the holdback on this car. He or she will usually understate this information to induce you to believe the dealer paid more for the vehicle than they actually paid.

Another relatively easy way to determine the lowest price most dealers will accept is to review the car advertisements in your local newspaper. Most dealers include ads for what I call "bait-and-switch" or "come-on" vehicles. They often list only one at the stated price, specifying the stock number of that vehicle. They include prices for the different models they sell, and this allows you to calculate their bottom-line price for the model you are seeking. The prices set forth in the "come-on" advertisements are as low as the dealers are likely to go for the vehicles listed. From car books or Internet sites, you can ascertain the dealer cost for the extra options you want and add those amounts to the advertised price. Even if the advertised car is an unacceptable color or not the exact model you wish to buy, you can still use the price of that vehicle as your guide. When salespeople mention higher prices, refocus their attention on the advertised car price. Force them to negotiate up from that figure, rather than down from their inflated figure. When you have talked them down to a number you find sufficiently close to the actual dealer cost, you have completed the first round.

Car Negotiating: Second Round

As soon as the salesperson gets your commitment to a specific price, the real bargaining games begin. For example, he will begin to write up the purchase contract and then disappear to consult with the "sales manager." After an absence of five to ten minutes, the sales person will return with a long face. He will indicate that the "sales manager" informed him that he had made a significant error that has resulted in a price below their actual cost. You will begin to feel sorry for the salesperson, who indicates that he almost lost his job because of this error. He will inform you that for several hundred dollars more, he should be able to convince the "sales manager" to approve the deal, even though it is still below the figure the manager expected. This is a ploy. For all you know, you are presently talking with the "sales manager," who had merely gotten something to eat or drink when he went into the other room. Don't allow this use of *Limited Authority* and the *Nibble Technique* to fleece you. Calmly restate your willingness to pay the previously agreed-upon price and nothing further.

If you are fortunate to reach a final agreement on the price you will pay, the sales person will write up a sales contract that contains pre-printed provisions that add on extra costs: vehicle transportation, dealer prep, and a "processing fee." You are normally expected to pay the transportation cost, since the dealer has been charged for that item. The other two charges, however, are negotiable. They are dealer add-ons that are designed to enhance their profit. Most dealers perform minimal service on new vehicles, yet they try to charge several hundred dollars for this work. The "processing fee" of $100 to $200 should have been reflected in the amount of dealer profit you agreed to provide above dealer cost. Despite the fact that these last two items are fictional sums to enhance dealer profit, it is difficult to eliminate them entirely. If you can get the dealer to drop one or reduce both, you have done well. These extra charges are already printed on the purchase agreement to be added to any price agreed upon, and it is hard to get dealers to delete pre-printed fee items.

Car Negotiating: Third Round

Only after you have agreed upon the final price and the degree to which you will pay for transportation costs, dealer prep, and processing, is it time to address the value of any trade-in you have. Try to avoid this issue until the end of your price negotiations. If salespeople are aware of your trade-in when they begin the negotiations, they will try to give you a less generous vehicle price. This allows them to look more generous when they make you an offer on your trade-in. By negotiating the final price before addressing your trade-in, you can determine the actual amount they are giving you for your current vehicle.

If you have negotiated a low price for the vehicle you are purchasing, car dealers are unlikely to be generous with respect to your trade-in. In most instances, they don't plan to sell your vehicle through their used car department, but intend to sell it through an automobile wholesale service. As part of your purchase preparation, you should determine both the wholesale and retail value of the vehicle you plan to trade in. Books and Internet services (such as www.edmunds.com and www.auto trader.com) can provide you with this information based on the make and model, the odometer mileage, and condition of your vehicle. Only when your car is in relatively good shape is the dealer likely to retain the car for resale through its used vehicle department. If you think it is going to do this, you should talk in terms of a figure at the low end of the retail value. Otherwise, you must anticipate a number based on the wholesale value.

If you think your vehicle is worth substantially more than dealers are willing to provide, you may decide to sell the vehicle yourself. Use the same aforementioned sources to determine the approximate retail value of your car. You can also read the used car ads in the local newspaper to see what other people are charging for similar vehicles. Select an asking price for your car that appears sufficiently reasonable to encourage prospective buyers to contact you once they see your advertisement. If the stated price is excessive, you will generate minimal interest. All in all, remember this: It may be a hassle to sell the vehicle yourself, but if you are able to obtain $1,000 or $2,000 more than the dealer offered, you will come out well ahead.

Car Negotiating: The Final Ploy

After you have negotiated the vehicle and trade-in value—and have signed a purchase agreement—a few unscrupulous dealers use one final ploy to increase the price. When you return to the dealership with your trade-in to pick up the car you have agreed to purchase, they look at your trade-in and "discover" some scratches and dings they had previously overlooked. They will ask you if these occurred after they determined the value of your trade-in and suggest that your vehicle is worth less than the price stated in the sales agreement. Unsophisticated buyers who are psychologically committed to the new car they are buying may succumb and agree to pay several hundred dollars more for the vehicle. Assuming the scratches and dings noted by the salesperson now were present when the dealer initially appraised the value of your trade-in, this ploy is not only unethical but unlawful. You have a legally enforceable purchase contract. If the dealer tries to use such a disingenuous game to alter the terms agreed upon, you can sue for breach of contract. When you encounter this tactic, emphasize the fact that the marks in question were there when the dealer originally evaluated that vehicle, and ask the dealer if he or she is refusing to honor the already executed binding purchased contract. At this point, dealers trying to use this ploy to obtain extra money will usually cave in and honor the sales price set forth in the purchase agreement.

If you personally hate to negotiate with car dealers, you can consider other options. One might be to visit a dealer that refuses to bargain. Saturn is the classic example. It sets firm prices for its cars and refuses to modify those figures. Many Mercedes dealers also have a no-negotiation policy. It would be painful for good negotiators to do business with these dealers, due to the apparent absence of any haggling. If you like to bargain, don't refuse to visit a Saturn or Mercedes dealer merely because of this policy. While they may not negotiate over the price of their cars, they will negotiate over the trade-in you are offering and sometimes over the price of optional equipment. If it is late in the model year or late in the month and they are trying to obtain incentive payments, they will be more generous regarding your trade-in. They may even offer you a good deal on particular options.

Vehicle Purchasing Services

If you absolutely hate to negotiate with car dealers and can't find one that sets a fair and firm price on each vehicle, you should consider the use of a vehicle-buying service. For a set fee—usually ranging from $100 to $400—you can retain a service that will negotiate prices with dealers in your area for the specific vehicle you want to buy. These services have purchasing power by virtue of the repeat business they can give to accommodating dealers, and they contact several dealers in an effort to obtain the optimal price. Once they collect the relevant information, they notify you of the prices they have negotiated with the dealers and guarantee those prices for a limited period of time.

Some of the national buying services include: (1) Auto-Advisor, (800) 326-1976, www.autoadvisor.com; (2) Car-Source, (800) 517-2277, www.carsource.com; and (3) Car-Bargains, (800) 475-7283, www.carbargains.org. A.A.R.P. members can avail themselves of that organization's Mature Advantage Auto Program, (800) 916-2887, to obtain beneficial dealer quotes. Check in your local area for similar services that may be available (such as CheckBook Magazine in the Washington, D.C. area). Other services available through the Internet include www.carsdirect.com and www.autonationdirect.com. A few less reputable dealers attempt to use the buyer-service price as a "bait-and-switch" tactic and try to convince you to purchase a more expensive model. Don't let them do this; and if they seem hesitant to honor the price they have already guaranteed, contact the buying service for assistance. If dealers refuse to honor the prices they have quoted, the buying services will do business elsewhere. Most car dealers are unwilling to risk the loss of this lucrative market.

Even if you decide to hire a car-buying service to obtain prices for you, don't hesitate to use the prices they give you to bargain with other dealers. Stop by other dealers in your area and ask them if they can beat the price you have already been guaranteed. This approach may allow you to save another couple of hundred dollars. Is it worth your going to another five or six dealers for such a saving? You may feel it is if this allows you to cover the cost of the buying service you employed.

Should you automatically do business with the dealer that has given you the lowest price for the car you want to buy? Not necessarily. Consider other relevant factors such as their reputation for providing good service, their proximity to your home in case you have to have warranty work performed there, and whether they provide a loaner vehicle if you have to leave the car overnight for repairs. You may find it well worth a couple of hundred extra dollars to do business with a dealer you trust in a location that is convenient.

Buying Used Cars

If you are seeking a used vehicle, rather than a new one, you can still obtain relevant price information through books available in bookstores and in public libraries. Internet sites can also be helpful (such as www.edmunds.com and www.autotrader.com). You can also review used car advertisements in local newspapers to get a good idea of vehicle prices. Should you purchase your vehicle from a used car dealer or an individual seller? This is a difficult question to answer. Dealers are more likely to have late model vehicles that are in good operating condition, and they usually set prices in the mid- to upper-*retail* range. They frequently include vehicle warranties. You can estimate dealer "cost" from the *wholesale* value for the cars you are considering since dealers have generally obtained their cars as trade-ins on new vehicles and they tend to use wholesale values when determining trade-in allowances (If pressed by new car buyers, dealers may have given them trade-in credit in the low *retail* range.) They are often willing to accept $300 to $500 above their base "cost."

Individual sellers usually hope to obtain prices in the low- to mid-retail range. Their price expectations are lower than used car dealers because their non-settlement alternative is the amount they could get on a trade-in toward new vehicles. Since dealers normally give new car buyers no more than the wholesale value of used vehicles (or occasionally the low retail value for late model cars), the private sellers consider the low- to mid-retail price range a good deal. Private sellers don't include personal warranties. On the other hand, if individual sellers are willing to provide you with the service records pertaining to their vehicles, you can decide whether they are in the shape you desire. In some instances, you can have the remaining portion of the original car warranties transferred to you.

How can you be sure you are not purchasing a vehicle that has a questionable background? Go to www.carfax .com and obtain a "lemon check." You enter the Vehicle Identification Number (VIN), and carfax.com provides you with the vehicle's history. Has it been in a major accident? Does the present odometer reading represent the vehicle's actual mileage? You should also ask to have your own mechanic inspect the vehicle before you purchase it. If the existing warranty will continue for a reasonable period of time, this should provide you with additional protection.

BUYING HOUSES

The first thing to decide when contemplating the purchase of a new house is the geographical area or areas in which you would consider living. Realtors like to say that three critical factors affect the value of houses: "location, location, and location." What areas are convenient in terms of your family members' schedules and commutes? While a neighborhood close to your place of employment may be more expensive than a community ten or fifteen miles away, the monetary cost of your commute and the frustration and time lost because of traffic may outweigh the higher house prices in the more convenient location. How good are the schools in each area? Ask every parent you know—colleagues at work, fellow congregants, and others who live in the area about the different school systems. Residing in a good public school district will cost more, but if you have children and care about the quality of education they will receive, you will end up spending that money for expensive private schools if you select a home in a weak district.

What type of house do you want—colonial, contemporary, split-level, other? How many bedrooms and bathrooms would you like to have? How big a yard? Would you be willing to live on a busy street or would you prefer a quieter setting? Would you like to find a neighborhood with a number of families who have young children or prefer an area with few youngsters? Is the proximity to grocery stores and other shopping centers important? What about closeness to religious and cultural institutions, and recreational facilities? To avoid false starts, answer these fundamental questions for yourself at the beginning.

Learn How to Determine Price

The next step is to gather information on house prices. In many areas, you can access large realty firms through the Internet, or go to www.housevalues.com and list.realestate

.yahoo.com and gather information concerning both recent sales and current listings. Public property records, accessible through Lexis/Nexis or through government deed records should provide price information pertaining to all houses in the neighborhoods you are contemplating, with the most recent sales transactions being the most relevant. Even if you are still living a distance away from the location to which you are moving, you can subscribe to the local newspaper and begin to review the real estate advertisements. You can also contact major real estate brokers and have them send you information about available houses. Before you ever begin your actual search for a new house, garner enough information so you know the value of different houses in the neighborhoods you like.

Knowledge is especially critical with respect to home buying for two reasons: First, this is a large expense. Intelligent Negotiating will save you and your family several thousand dollars. Second, you may enter a seller's market in which houses are moving quickly. If you don't appreciate the value of a particular house, it may be sold before you even begin the serious discussions.

Contact Seller and Buyer Real Estate Agents

If you simply contact real estate firms, you will normally deal with seller agents who have a number of listings they hope to show you. While most real estate agents try to be fair to both buyers and sellers, these individuals are going to be paid a share of the sale price by their clients, and they feel a greater loyalty to those individuals. To avoid this possible conflict, many home buyers now retain their own *buyer agents*. (To obtain information on buyer agents nationwide, you can go into www.finderhome .com.) These are individuals who work primarily or exclusively for purchasers. They have to satisfy their buying clients, or they don't get paid. They thus have a real incentive to locate houses in your price range that satisfy your stated needs. If they are able to locate a house you like and you decide to buy it, they act as your bargaining agent vis-a-vis the selling agents. They are usually remunerated from a share of the sales commission. They can help you find good financing and assist you through the closing. Through Internet sites such as www.lending tree.com, you can get several lending institutions to compete against one another to obtain your business.

It is important to remember that buyer and seller agents only get paid when they are able to procure house deals. As a result, even seller agents are not completely loyal to their own clients. I have encountered a number of real estate agents who were willing to indicate the degree to which particular sellers were anxious to relocate. Or they have noted that the sellers had already purchased another home and had a bridge loan that was due within the next sixty days. Several have told me that their clients would be willing to reduce their asking price by significant amounts, and a couple have even indicated that the sellers were being transferred by business firms that would subsidize the sale of their homes to allow them to lower the price and sell quickly. I doubt the sellers were aware of the degree of candor evidenced in these disclosures. I have also seen buyer agents suggest to sellers that their clients would be willing to pay more than they were presently offering.

House Negotiating: First Round

If you are planning to visit a new area for a few days to try to purchase a house, ask several realtors to send you listing information through the mail, e-mail transmission, or by fax. This allows you to become familiar with the general market before you arrive. Once you arrive, try to visit as many different properties as you can during the first day or two. This allows you to appreciate the houses that are available and the prices being sought. Ask the realtors a lot of questions. Have housing prices been increasing or decreasing over the past twelve months? How long does the average house remain on the market before sale? What are the current mortgage rates available in this area?

Once you have narrowed your search to certain houses, continue asking questions. Ask realtors how close to asking prices most recent sales have been? In some areas of the country, selling prices are very close to asking prices, while in other areas they may be 5, 10, or even 15 percent below asking prices. When you decide to make an offer on the house, privately ask the selling agent what he or she thinks would entice the seller. More often than you think, agents will suggest a figure below the asking price that they think would be accepted. How much do you want this particular property? If you have found your dream house, and no other home like it is available, you may have to pay a premium. If, on the other hand, other similar properties are available and you are willing to look elsewhere, you can afford to gamble.

Don't try to talk sellers into lower prices by denigrating their house. They have probably lived in that dwelling for a number of years and have become attached to it. If you start telling them what is wrong with their house, they are likely to react with hostility and may even withdraw from the negotiation process. You are better off telling them how much you like their house. After all, if you thought it wasn't nice, why would you be thinking of offering them thousands of dollars for it? Once you have indicated how much you want to purchase their house, you can politely mention the aspects that might warrant a decrease in the price they are asking. If the interior or exterior must be painted, how much would this cost? If the carpeting needs to be replaced or the floors have to be refinished, what would this cost? While you may try to use such information to generate price reductions, you must remember that the sellers probably considered these factors when setting their asking price. If you soften your discussions regarding these issues, the sellers are more likely to listen objectively and reevaluate the need to reduce the price they are seeking.

Some sellers try to whipsaw buyers against one another. As soon as they get an offer from one person, they have their agent contact the other parties who have recently expressed an interest in the house. They hope to generate a bidding war that will increase the price. To avoid this possibility, make an offer with a severely limited duration, say, good for a maximum of twenty-four or forty-eight hours. I have seen prospective buyers make offers that were good only until the evening of the date they were made. This forces sellers to decide how much they are willing to gamble. If they are anxious—particularly if their house has been on the market for several months— they are likely to move quickly. Most people are hesitant to reject a *sure gain* when they may end up with no sale.

In most instances, your initial offer generates a counteroffer from the seller. They may be asking $250,000 and you offer $230,000. They then counter with a request for $240,000, and you respond with a new offer of $235,000.

Before you know it, you have agreed to a sale in the area of $237,500. Since parties tend to move toward the center from their opening positions, you should carefully consider what your opening offer should be. You want to start as far away from the asking price as you can—while still generating real interest in the sellers. If your offer is insultingly low, you will offend the sellers and diminish the likelihood of a counteroffer. On the other hand, if you begin with too generous an offer, it may be readily accepted and you would experience "buyer's remorse." You would be displeased with the price and try to get out of the deal or obtain a price reduction as the closing date approaches.

When you sit down with your family and your buying agent to plan your opening offer, look at the asking price and the price you would like to pay. Try to select an offer that places your goal near the middle. Imagine where the seller would be likely to counter, and plan your next offer to keep your target number in the middle. If the seller makes a counter that is less generous than you anticipated, you can moderate your new offer. If, however, the seller comes down further than you expected, you may still wish to make only a slight increase in your counter to see how anxious the seller may be.

While you are making offers and counteroffers, the parties are usually discussing various items that may be included in the sale of the house, such as the drapes, certain furnishings, and various appliances. Would you be willing to forego these items for a lower price? In most cases, unless you already have these items, you are smart to increase your offer if the seller is willing to include them. The extra cost to you will normally be substantially below what it would cost to purchase these items new. Since most sellers have no interest in taking these house-specific items with them to their new location, they are willing to give you a good deal.

House Negotiating: Second Round

Once the parties achieve mutually acceptable terms, they sign a formal purchase contract. Do not make the mistake of assuming the deal is final at this point. You still have to agree upon a closing date, and you may have a time frame that differs substantially from that of your counterpart. As the buyer, you will want to have the house inspected to be certain everything is in working order, particularly if the house is more than a few years old. The realtor can help you find a reputable firm to hire for a professional inspection. You should normally not ask the selling agent, because he or she would have an interest in recommending someone who is unlikely to find too many problems. Ask a buying agent or a disinterested selling agent to suggest the names of several inspection services.

House inspectors almost always discover some problem areas. These have to be addressed before closing. Some buyers use house inspectors as the basis for the *Nibble Technique* discussed in chapter 6. They demand significant price reductions based on the problems that have been discovered. Some deliberately select inspection firms that have a reputation for finding difficulties. Even if everything is currently working, they point out the obvious fact that the roof is now fifteen years old, the kitchen appliances are ten years old, and the heating and cooling system may have to be replaced within the next four to five years. These facts should have been apparent when they initially examined the house, and these considerations were presumably reflected in the purchase price. Sellers confronted by such claims should usually refuse to make price reductions.

If the inspector you hire finds some unexpected difficulties, sit down with the real estate agent and the seller and try to work out a fair arrangement. The seller may reduce the price accordingly or agree to fix up the problems before—or even after—the closing date. The seller may agree to place a specified amount of the purchase price in an escrow account to allow you to take care of the necessary repairs. Sellers who think that buyers are being greedy can agree to have the work done by their own people. This allows them to get the estimates and select the people to do the work. It also forces the buyers to indicate whether they really want the work done. I have seen buyers demand price reductions to permit them to have "critical" repairs done—only to have the buyers leave those items untouched for several years after they move in. They were merely using these items as a tool to obtain price reductions and didn't really care whether those problems were fixed.

If buyers and/or sellers expect difficulty as the closing date approaches, they should allow their real estate agents to bring the deal to a successful conclusion. Buyers or sellers who fear last-minute problems at the closing can send their agents to the meeting with the necessary sales papers and their power of attorney, and not show up at the actual meeting. They can make themselves unavailable and force their counterparts to decide how much they are willing to hold up the final deals.

When potential difficulties arise in real estate transactions, it is important to remember that *both sides* want the deal to be consummated. The sellers are relocating and want to be rid of their house, and the buyers need a new home into which to move. If both parties can remain civil and deal with problems in an intelligent manner, they will almost always agree upon mutually acceptable solutions.

Summary Points

- Doing your homework before you enter discussions on a car or house purchase will make the experience a more pleasant and more profitable one.

- When buying a new car, first decide which makes or models would suit your needs. Then determine the actual dealer cost of those vehicles, and use that as your base negotiating price.

- Be prepared to negotiate the dealer profit, and the cost of options, as well as the transportation costs, dealer prep, and processing fees as the "sales manager" uses the "Nibble" Technique to obtain further price concessions from you. Only after you do that should you address the value of your trade-in (if applicable).

- When buying a house, contact seller and buyer real estate agents to obtain information about the cost of available houses in the areas in which you would like to live.

- Plan your house-buying negotiation strategy carefully, and be prepared for post-agreement bargaining.

CHAPTER 11

SITUATION 3: NEGOTIATING WITH REPAIR SHOPS

T oo often we consumers find ourselves at a disadvantage when we have to negotiate with car dealers over vehicle repairs or with repair shops over appliance breakdowns. We are usually not experts with respect to the machinery in question, and at times our lack of sophistication allows unscrupulous mechanics to take advantage of us. Since we are unlikely to develop the knowledge required to preclude unnecessary repair work, we should be able to use our negotiation skills to minimize the possibility of such events.

FIND A REPUTABLE REPAIR SHOP

If you are not facing an emergency situation, you should first ask friends to recommend trustworthy vehicle or appliance service shops. If you live near a metropolitan area, you may be able to look in a local consumer magazine for ratings of repair establishments. A call to the local Better Business Bureau can let you know whether it has received significant complaints about the firms you are thinking of using.

DESCRIBE YOUR PROBLEM AS SPECIFICALLY AS POSSIBLE

When you take your vehicle or appliance to the shop, try to appear as knowledgeable as possible. You can start by specifically describing the problem you wish to have addressed. If you merely indicate to the mechanic, for example, that your car is not working properly or the refrigerator is making a strange noise, he or she may assume that you don't understand how your machine is supposed to work. On the other hand, if you can explain the precise nature of the malfunction (for example, "The transmission is slipping when shifting from second into third gear" or "The freezer compartment has not been maintaining a sufficiently low temperature"), you accomplish two objectives: First, you make it easier for the repairperson to diagnose the underlying problem. Second, the more this person thinks you know about the repair to be performed, the less likely he or she is to take advantage of you.

AGREE ON THE EXACT WORK TO BE DONE AND THE SPECIFIC PRICE FOR THAT WORK

Once the repairperson has examined the vehicle or the appliance and developed an understanding of the problem, be sure to ask for a detailed explanation. What is the precise problem, and what should be done to correct it? Never be ashamed to admit your inability to understand the repairperson's technical language. Ask them to explain using terms that a layperson can understand. If you still have difficulty comprehending the exact problem, ask for an even simpler explanation. Good mechanics are usually able to describe the problem and its solution in terms any of us can understand.

After you have nailed down the problem to be corrected, ask for a precise estimate of the cost. Have the repairperson detail the work to be performed—the parts to be replaced and the labor involved. You want an estimate that will apprise you of the exact cost involved. If they only provide general estimates, the work may end up costing far more than you anticipated. Once they give you a specific estimate, the shop is bound to that figure unless you subsequently authorize more work based upon the discovery of unexpected problems.

If you find the estimate high, don't hesitate to ask about other options that may be available to you. Could the part in question be repaired instead of replaced? If you have to have a replacement part, could the shop obtain a used part from a junk dealer or a rebuilt part from a reputable firm? These options can save you a great deal of money and depending on the part, may last just as long as a new part.

Don't hesitate to ask repairpeople: "Is that the best price you can give me?" They may be willing to substitute less expensive parts or offer you a lower labor cost to get your business. This is especially likely if business has been slow lately. Such a polite inquiry could save you 25 percent or more. If you would like to have this shop do the repair work but have received a better estimate from somewhere else, don't hesitate to mention the lower bid. This shop may be willing to match that price.

If the estimate you have obtained is still excessive, telephone or visit other repair shops. If possible, take the car or appliance with you to give shop personnel the opportunity to examine it. They may give you a different diagnosis that saves you money. If your car is not running or the appliance is too large to take to the shop, some repair people are willing to visit your house to examine it. If they are hesitant to come in person, you can describe exactly what the first shop said is wrong and what must be done to correct the problem and ask for a second opinion. Another shop may have less expensive parts available or charge less for labor. This effort may save you $50 to $100 on an appliance and possibly hundreds of dollars on a vehicle.

Repair or Replace?

If repairs are going to be expensive, would you be better off purchasing another vehicle or appliance? Don't give up on your old car or refrigerator too quickly. A $500 or $750 repair to your car transmission or $150 repair to your refrigerator compressor may enable you to drive the car or use the refrigerator for another four to five years. If the car or refrigerator is otherwise in good shape, the current repair expense may be a rational investment. On the other hand, if your car or appliance is old and you are likely to encounter future repair problems, you may find purchasing a new or used vehicle or a new refrigerator more cost effective.

Don't make the mistake of continuing to throw good money after bad simply because of the amounts you have already paid for repairs to your present car or appliance. Such an *escalation of commitment* can entangle you in a losing venture. Assess whether the car or appliance has become too expensive to maintain. Once it becomes too costly, look for a substitute no matter how much you have already put into this one. If you retain the car or appliance after the point of diminishing returns, you will not only waste good money, you also lessen the chance that you will ultimately purchase as good a replacement model. When you evaluate the amount you have spent on the old car or appliance, you often decrease the amount you are willing to pay toward a new car or appliance, resulting in the purchase of a lower quality replacement.

GET IT IN WRITING

Once you decide to have the repair work performed, obtain the following: First, ask for a written form indicating the exact work to be done containing a specific price quote. Second, ask the shop to specify the warranty period for the work being done. Many automobile and appliance shops now guarantee replacement parts for as long as you own the vehicle or appliance. Be sure to have them indicate whether the warranty covers parts *and* labor. If it only covers replacement parts, you will often discover that, should the new part fail, the labor cost to replace the part is nearly as expensive as the original repair.

Never give repair shops expansive authority to perform extra work they discover once they get into the current job. The authority you give them can be used (and often is) to substantially increase your final bill. Don't hesitate to authorize minor work that doesn't exceed a modest amount (such as $50), with the shop being obliged to call you and obtain specific approval for more extensive work.

BEYOND NEGOTIATING: DON'T BE TAKEN BY UNSCRUPULOUS REPAIR SHOPS

If a vehicle or appliance part is being replaced, ask the shop to give you the old part once it has been removed. Many shops do this as a matter of course. Even if they do not, they should not hesitate to do so when requested. If you have any doubts about the shop's reputation, secretly mark the old part in an area not easily seen by others. When they give you the part that was removed, you can look for your mark to be sure they have not given you an old part from another car or appliance. They may have simply repaired your existing part and charged you for a new one, as they did for a friend of mine who supposedly had to have an expensive alternator replaced in his car. He marked his alternator and left the car with the dealer. When he returned to the shop later that day, they gave him the "old alternator." It was not the one that had been in his vehicle. He discovered that the shop had repaired his old alternator and charged him for a new one!

When car dealers are required to perform warranty work, they occasionally try to make up for their lost revenues by finding additional work that should be done. A few years ago, my wife and I took our recently purchased car to the dealer for regular service. During the day, the shop called to say that our brake rotors were a bit worn and needed to be resurfaced at a cost of over $100. Since the brakes seemed to be working fine, we declined this suggestion. Although the dealer tried to suggest that this decision might cause an accident if the brakes subsequently failed, we still refused to have the work done. We later discovered that the manufacturer had instructed its dealers to replace the brake pads in our model due to unusually rapid wear. The dealer was required to perform this work for the manufacturer and sought to make up for the lost revenue by inducing customers to pay to have the rotors resurfaced when this procedure was not necessary given the limited mileage on the vehicle.

Even when you don't seek out repair work, you may be taken by unscrupulous individuals. Classic examples include scammers who ring your doorbell and inform you that they are roofers or driveway repair people who are working in the neighborhood. They offer to reseal your roof or driveway for a bargain price. If you accept their offer, they are likely to cover your shingles or driveway with a worthless solution that may briefly look impressive, but have no lasting impact. If you are considering having these services performed, retain a reputable local firm and get an estimate before you commission any work.

Another scam involves people traveling on out-of-state trips who, when they stop for gas, are told by unscrupulous service station mechanics that their shock absorbers or brakes are leaking. Such mechanics squirt shock absorber or brake fluid on the ground beneath your car while you are visiting the restroom or buying food and drinks, and show you the "leaking" fluid when you return to your car. They look concerned and suggest that further travel with the vehicle in this condition could be highly dangerous. To avoid this common scam, never leave your car unattended when you stop at out-of-state service stations for gas. If you are alone, remain with the car while your tank is being filled. Once that task is finished, pull to the side of the station to visit the bathroom or to purchase food. If you are traveling with others, have someone stay by the car while the others visit the facilities or buy food. If they know that someone is watching, you won't be cheated this way.

If you suspect that an out-of-state mechanic might be telling the truth about a possible shock absorber or brake leak, take your car to the local car dealer and ask for an inspection. If the service station mechanic was trying to scam you, the car dealer service personnel are likely to wipe off the fluid sprayed on the shock absorbers or brake lines and send you on your way. If you actually have a problem, the dealer can confirm that fact and give you an estimate for the work.

SUMMARY POINTS

- Negotiation skills can minimize the possibility of unfairly high repair bills.
- Find a reputable shop. Describe your problems as specifically as possible.
- Agree on the exact work to be done and the specific price for that work.
- Get written work orders containing the exact price for the work and stating any applicable warranties.
- Know when escalating repair costs make it economically preferable to replace the malfunctioning vehicle or appliance.
- Don't let repair shops or repair persons charge you for unauthorized or unnecessary work.

PREPARING TO NEGOTIATE: A PREPARATION FORM

The Negotiation Preparation Checklist leads you through a series of questions designed to ensure thorough preparation in any upcoming bargaining situation. Ask yourself how you would answer each question. What would your ultimate bargaining objectives be, and how would you plan to get from your opening position to where you hope to end up?

NEGOTIATION PREPARATION FORM

1. Your Bottom Line: Determine the minimum terms you would accept given your Best Alternative to a Negotiated Agreement (BATNA). Don't forget to include the monetary and non-monetary transaction costs associated with both settlement and non-settlement.

2. Your Aspiration Level: Identify the best results you think you could possibly achieve. Be certain your aspiration level is sufficiently high. Don't begin a negotiation until you have mentally solidified your ultimate objective with respect to *each item* that is to be exchanged.

3. Your Counterpart's Bottom Line: Estimate your counterpart's bottom line, being certain to include the monetary and non-monetary transaction costs when estimating the external alternatives that may be available to your opponent.

4. Your Counterpart's Aspiration Level: Estimate your counterpart's bargaining objectives, trying to use his or her value system.

5. Your Arguments: Plan support for your position with respect to *each issue* to be discussed. Prepare logical explanations supporting your strengths and anticipate the ways you might minimize possible positional weaknesses.

6. Your Counterpart's Arguments: Anticipate your opponent's support for his or her claims with respect to the various issues. Prepare innovative counterarguments that can you use to challenge the claims you expect your opponent to make.

7. Your Planned Opening Position: Always request more or offer less than you hope to achieve. Prepare rational explanations to support each component of your principled opening offer.

8. Information You Seek: Determine what you plan to elicit from your opponent during the Information Exchange to determine his or her underlying needs, interests, and objectives. What information-seeking questions do you anticipate using?

9. Information You Plan to Offer: Decide what information you are willing to disclose to your opponent during the Information Exchange and how you plan to divulge it. How do you plan to prevent the disclosure of your sensitive information (*"Blocking Techniques"*)?

10. Your Negotiation Strategy: Plan your anticipated concession pattern carefully to disclose only the information you intend to divulge and prepare principled explanations to support each planned concession.

11. Your Opponent's Negotiation Strategy and Your Countermeasures: Predict what your opponent's strategy will be and how can you neutralize your opponent's strengths and exploit his or her weaknesses.

12. Your Negotiating Techniques: Decide what tactics you plan to use to advance your interests. (Be prepared to vary them and to combine them for optimal impact.)

13. Your Opponent's Negotiating Techniques: Anticipate the techniques you expect your counterpart to use, and decide how you might counter those tactics.

NOTES

Introduction

1. Daniel Goleman, *Emotional Intelligence* (New York: Bantam, 1995).

Chapter 1

1. Gerald Williams, *Legal Negotiation and Settlement* (St. Paul, MN: West Publishing, 1983): 18-39.

2. Andrea Kupfer Schneider, "Shattering Negotiation Myths: Empirical Evidence on the Effectiveness of Negotiation Style," *Harvard Negotiation Law Review* 7 (2002): 143, 167.

3. James G. Sammataro, "Business and Brotherhood, Can They Coincide? A Search into Why Black Athletes Do Not Hire Black Agents," *Howard Law Journal 42* (1999): 535.

4. Charles B. Craver, "Race and Negotiation Performance," *Dispute Resolution Magazine 8* (Fall 2001): 22.

5. Nicky Marone, *Women and Risk* (New York: St. Martin's Press, 1992): 42-45; Valerie Miner and Helen Longino, *Competition: A Feminist Taboo?* (New York: Feminist Press, 1987): 50-55.

6. Ian Ayres, "Fair Driving, Gender and Race Discrimination in Retail Car Negotiations," *Harvard Law Review 104* (1991): 817.

7. Charles B. Craver and David W. Barnes, "Gender, Risk Taking, and Negotiation Performance," *Michigan Journal of Gender & Law 5* (1999): 328-333.

Chapter 2

1. Roger Fisher and William Ury, *Getting to Yes* (New York: Houghton Mifflin, 1981): 101-111.

2. Amos Tversky and Daniel Kahneman, "The Framing of Decisions and the Psychology of Choice," *Science 211* (1981): 453.

Chapter 4

1. Jo-Ellan Dimitrius and Mark Mazzarella, *Reading People* (New York: Random House, 1998).

2. Desmond Morris, *Bodytalk* (New York: Crown Publishing, 1994).

3. Paul Ekman, *Telling Lies* (New York: W. W. Norton, 1992).

4. Robert Bastress and Joseph Harbaugh, *Interviewing, Counseling, and Negotiating* (Boston: Little, Brown, 1990): 493.

5. Robert Bastress and Joseph Harbaugh, *Interviewing, Counseling, and Negotiating* (Boston: Little, Brown, 1990): 483.

Chapter 5

1. Robert Bastress and Joseph Harbaugh, *Interviewing, Counseling, and Negotiating* (Boston: Little, Brown, 1990): 439-440.
2. Manuel J. Smith, *When I Say No, I Feel Guilty* (New York: Bantam Books, 1975).

Chapter 6

1. Joel Chandler Harris, *The Complete Tales of Uncle Remus,* compiled by Richard Chase (Boston: Houghton Mifflin, 1955): 875.

Chapter 8

1. Robert Axelrod, *The Evolution of Cooperation* (New York: Basic Books, 1984).
2. Robert Axelrod, *The Evolution of Cooperation* (New York: Basic Books, 1984): 109-124.

INDEX

ABOUT THE AUTHOR

Charles Craver is the Leroy S. Merrifield Research Professor of Law at George Washington University in Washington, D.C., where he teaches legal negotiating. He has taught more than 60,000 lawyers and businesspeople negotiation skills in workshops conducted throughout the United States, Canada, Mexico, Puerto Rico, England, and the People's Republic of China. He is the author of *Effective Legal Negotiation and Settlement* (4th Edition, 2001; Lexis/Nexis), coauthor of *Alternative Dispute Resolution: The Advocate's Perspective* (2nd Edition, 2001; Lexis/Nexis), and author or coauthor of eight other books and numerous professional publications. Craver previously practiced law in San Francisco, and is currently a negotiation consultant, mediator, and arbitrator. He lives in Washington, D.C., with his wife.